# Madness: a form of love

by Max J. Lewy

*- Published by Max J. Lewy*

*All rights reserved. No part of this book may be reproduced, stored in a retrieval system, or transmitted in any form, or by any means, electronic, mechanical, photocopying, recording or otherwise, without prior permission of the author.*

*Copyright © 2018 Max J. Lewy
All rights reserved*

**PAPERBACK PRINT BOOK ISBN NUMBERS:**

ISBN 10:   1986974324
ISBN 13:   978-1986974325

Madness: a form of love

For R.W

## ABOUT THE AUTHOR

Born crown-prince of Hell, aka the dreary and poverty-stricken South Wales valleys, Max J. Lewy (1983 – ....) spent an eternity in limbo before arising to take his proper and rightful throne. As he was scaling the almighty steps of the empyreal palace, called the Word, a beast most foul and uncouth, in the garb of a physician, cast itself upon him. The chemical-wielding barbarian known to the slumbering masses respectfully as a 'psychiatrist' slew by dint of overwhelming idiocy what a million petty hours of boredom (and computer games) had only mildly arrested. He lingers on merely as a memento to this unhappy happening, worshipping and picking over the ever-fragrant corpses of his spiritual ancestors, such as the great and lonely Friedrich Nietzsche, the wily Leo Strauss, the exquisite fanatic Yukio Mishima, and the electrocuted yet graceful Townes Van Zandt.

Max J. Lewy can be contacted at:
max.lewy@outlook.com

## ACKNOWLEDGMENTS

Many thanks to all my friends and family for their support, and all the great thinkers and critics of psychiatric cruelty who have nourished and consoled me over the last decade. These include but are not limited to and in no particular order: my mother Helen Lewy, my brother Alex Lewy, my cousin Benjamin Lewy, Seth Farber PHD., Julia Padfield, Kim Van Breda, Dr. Peter Breggin, Vijay Vaghela, Joanna Moncrieff, the late Dr. Thomas Szasz, Daniel Carter, Stephen S. Lawrence, Ben Turner, Samm Sheh, Russell Currie, Stephen Molyneux, Ted Chabasinski, Jim Gottstein, Dion Zessin, Cheryl Prax, Elvin F. Verdad, Jonathon Fisherman, Sara Arenson, Ben Goldacre, Momohjimoh AbulGafar, Matthew Dennis, Frank Blankenship, Scott Hart, Michele Koppinger, Lauren Tenney, Barbara Barrett, Steven Kivari, Marilyn Welton, Jenny Cranston, Melda Baptista, David Carmichael, Brent Potter, Rob Wilkinson, Ian Harris, everyone at Elim Church and in Blackwood Poetry group. May the fight continue.

"One must still have chaos inside oneself to give birth to a dancing star"

— F.W. Nietzsche

## CONTENTS

| Sr.No. | Title | Pg. No. |
|---|---|---|
| 1 | What My Madness Brings | 1 |
| 2 | Madness Is a Form Of Love | 3 |
| 3 | Community Nurse | 4 |
| 4 | Write To Survive | 5 |
| 5 | Golden Boy | 6 |
| 6 | Gentility Without Joy | 8 |
| 7 | Sacred Jungle Of Dreams | 9 |
| 8 | Just More Meds | 10 |
| 9 | Unkempt Stars | 11 |
| 10 | Lobotomized The Beast | 12 |
| 11 | Tiny Little Pill | 15 |
| 12 | Born Unfurled | 16 |
| 13 | The Gondolier | 17 |
| 14 | Ben | 18 |
| 15 | Your Apocalypse | 20 |
| 16 | Through A Window Paine | 22 |
| 17 | 'Mad Community', or, A Small Bird Willows On The Branch | 23 |
| 18 | Night Stroll | 24 |
| 19 | The Day I Gave Up On Mankind | 25 |
| 20 | Ode To Lunacy | 27 |
| 21 | Doctors And Madmen | 28 |
| 22 | City Sage | 29 |
| 23 | Little Superman | 31 |
| 24 | Surreptitious Smile | 33 |
| 25 | Vaccine Against Love | 34 |
| 26 | My Prospective Ubermensch | 35 |
| 27 | Beautiful Id | 36 |
| 28 | Arising Aurora | 37 |
| 29 | Love's Little Vandal | 38 |
| 30 | The Phantom | 39 |
| 31 | Gaudy Grin | 41 |
| 32 | Shrinking Between The Lines | 42 |
| 33 | Neptune's Daughter | 43 |
| 34 | In The Garden | 44 |
| 35 | The Lilac Lighthouse | 45 |

| 36 | The Gravest Sin | 46 |
| --- | --- | --- |
| 37 | Non-Coercive World | 48 |
| 38 | Close To One's Chest | 49 |
| 39 | Rumination on Self-Assertion | 50 |
| 40 | God Is Inside | 51 |
| 41 | Courting Fiasco | 53 |
| 42 | The Death Of A Flower Girl | 54 |
| 43 | Madness: a form of love | 55 |
| 44 | On The Notion Of 'Effort' As A Virtue For Life | 56 |
| 45 | Aurora Borealis | 57 |
| 46 | O Grim Lord, Why Art Thou So Blue? | 59 |
| 47 | You Live On | 60 |
| 48 | Penning Poems | 61 |
| 49 | Dionysus On The Dole | 62 |
| 50 | Beneath The Bell Jar | 64 |
| 51 | All Quiet On The Frontal Lobes | 65 |
| 52 | Psychiatric Scapegoat | 66 |
| 53 | The Voice Of A Babe | 68 |
| 54 | Picked | 69 |
| 55 | Sunrise, unrise! | 70 |
| 56 | Silenced Song | 71 |
| 57 | Brain Is Broken | 73 |
| 58 | Sullen Sun | 75 |
| 59 | Mad Transgressions (Put Acid In the Pope's Woopie-cushion!) | 77 |
| 60 | The Failure Of The Enlightenment For Man's Moral Education | 79 |
| 61 | The Morgue | 80 |
| 62 | My Struggle: The Triumph Of The (W)ill | 81 |
| 63 | Zeus Beware | 82 |
| 64 | Even Paper | 83 |
| 65 | A Good-Natured Malignancy | 84 |
| 66 | Birthday Barometer | 85 |
| 67 | You | 86 |
| 68 | The Turin Horse | 87 |
| 69 | Medusa's Uncle | 88 |
| 70 | Britain Finally Gets Up Off Her Knees | 89 |
| 71 | The Only Race | 90 |
| 72 | Creepy Conscience | 91 |
| 73 | 3/22: The Seeding | 92 |

| 74 | End In Fire | 93 |
| 75 | Teenage Trends | 95 |
| 76 | Professional Licences | 96 |
| 77 | The Infowarrior | 97 |
| 78 | Stockholm Syndrome | 98 |
| 79 | Piloting The Soul | 99 |
| 80 | The Moon In June | 100 |
| 81 | Blueberry Bodhisattva | 102 |
| 82 | Madness Is Everything | 103 |
| 83 | Hearing From History | 104 |
| 84 | Care Plan Is A Cruel Plan | 105 |
| 85 | Bon Appetite | 106 |
| 86 | The Neon Isle of Inner City | 107 |
| 87 | Save a care and don't help, don't even help the helpers | 108 |
| 88 | Hurled | 110 |
| 89 | Lunar Portal | 111 |
| 90 | The Wheels of Samsara | 112 |
| 91 | Gus | 113 |
| 92 | Midnight Misgivings | 114 |
| 93 | Anthem For Drugged Youth | 115 |
| 94 | Crimson Sails | 116 |
| 95 | Sturdy Stalwart Stance | 117 |
| 96 | The Tryst | 118 |
| 97 | Meeting With The Most Beautiful Angel | 119 |
| 98 | Penance | 120 |
| 99 | Visions Of My Funeral | 121 |
| 100 | Sure Sailing | 122 |
| 101 | S.S., Smiley Squadron | 123 |
| 102 | Beauty Of The Word | 124 |
| 103 | Crest Of Sorrow | 125 |
| 104 | Common Enemy | 126 |
| 105 | Hymn To The Medicated Messiah | 127 |
| 106 | All I Can Really Manage | 128 |
| 107 | Cacophonous Coffin | 130 |
| 108 | Dreams | 131 |
| 109 | Wholly Marginal | 133 |
| 110 | Small Truculences | 135 |
| 111 | Privilege And Iniquity | 136 |
| 112 | A Power-Above | 138 |

| 113 | Our Own Great Missed Opportunity | 140 |
| 114 | Rose Towards The Sun | 141 |
| 115 | He Cometh No More | 142 |
| 116 | Become Mentally-Ill And Make a Quick Buck | 143 |
| 117 | A Universal Song | 147 |
| 118 | Pill Puppet Poet | 148 |
| 119 | Grief | 149 |
| 120 | Cherub Rock | 151 |
| 121 | Crystal Carrion | 153 |
| 122 | The Great Invisible | 154 |
| 123 | A Parable, 'Man And Truth' | 155 |
| 124 | Orchid | 156 |
| 125 | Gemini Asunder | 157 |
| 126 | Unmetabolizable Angst | 158 |
| 127 | Never mind | 159 |
| 128 | Note To The Homeless | 161 |
| 129 | "Schizophrenia" Will Demean Ya | 162 |
| 130 | Asylum Chums | 163 |
| 131 | The Mask Is No More | 165 |
| 132 | Holy Land | 166 |
| 133 | My Lost Israel | 167 |
| 134 | The Call Of Duty | 168 |
| 135 | Thoughts Of The Unborn | 169 |
| 136 | Mountain Path | 171 |
| 137 | Rain Panegyric | 172 |
| 138 | Tears Of Solace | 174 |
| 139 | Monsoon Bride (Or, "I Refuse To Hurt") | 175 |
| 140 | Backstreet Buddha (Lets Fall A Jewel...) | 177 |
| 141 | Relics | 178 |
| 142 | Blitzcare | 179 |
| 143 | He Strove | 180 |
| 144 | Paralysed By The Prick Of A Dovetail | 181 |
| 145 | Lost In The Fray | 183 |
| 146 | Rivers Of Eternity (for R.W.) | 184 |

\* \* \* \* \* \*

Madness: a form of love

Max J. Lewy

## What My Madness Brings

Confession is not in my disposition,
Humility isn't for me.
I have too much accusation,
To stoop to mutual sympathy-
To offer up in supplication,
My rightful property,
Or stand before adjudication,
Bowing my head as if I were guilty.
Even if I too have failed in perfection...
It is probably due to thee.

Moreover, it is for the criminals to come forth,
Not for me to bring them to justice.
After all they've done to murder my mirth,
I deserve a medal for my mere lingering existence.

So I don't come before you humbly...
All stuttering, all mumbly.
And though I might like to play the minstrel knight,
I am not one who is made for easy delight.
Though I may often seem only to want to punish grumpily,
In reality, by beating this proverbial shield of tin,
I beseech you to alter course that we may yet win.

Hear me now! I am not casting a stone,
Let alone the first. 'tis no violence to merely intone:
I just searchingly bemoan.
(In a forum less likely to get me in the bin thrown)

Like a damaged bird, or dragon hoarding ruby
Rings with its lovely clipped wings,
That from pride and pity
Still breathes fire and sings;
Thus my Judgement Bell loudly

Yet subtly, insidiously dings-

May whatever God lurks see that this tragic ditty
Your lackadaisical consciences sorely stings!

..For the sake of society..
..for the sake of your souls..
..for the sake of your sins..

Pray: Do not refuse me, still less consider me an enemy;
It is only with repentance that true redemption begins.

..Not before me..
..But before each other..
..And, moreover, within..

Oh I know you're working hard, that you've been busy...
But save one more glance for what my "madness" brings!-
If you listen or sleep through it soundly, this is still my duty.
What do I care if you balk or cringe?
Poets - ONLY poets - are PERMITTED to be crazy.

Thus do I sombrely rant and rave,
For in these verses lurks the bitter reconciliation I crave.

# Madness Is A Form Of Love

A lunatic, according to its true definition, is he who is possessed by an amorous intoxication with the moon: In other words, with the unconscious motive principle of all Life on earth. To others, he can be identified as he who dances to, what is to them, an inaudible, non-existent tune. In reality, his jig is as inwardly necessary as are the fields of hops at their annual time of rebirth. Meddling with its natural course can cause tidal waves big enough to drown a seahorse.

For he still carries the strength, that others have lost, for wild flights of ecstasy, home-brewed by his own gallant imagination. He would repudiate the very dirt we walk on if it stirs not the desire in his breast. But in his proud pursuit of self-realization comes abandonment to self-revelation, to unflinching honesty in a world of war and deception, that makes him the naked-infant-on-a-doorstep target of all well-trained busy-bodies, conformity enforcers. How they long to divorce him from the warm light of Nature's hearth! In his beautiful simplicity, this Noble Savage disregards the wisdom of Christ's time-honoured tale, and asks against the entire tide of human history, against the insipid simulacra of everyday thoughts and gestures, against the stupid, iron-clad rules of the State, against the nonsensical taboos of society, against every bitter betrayal that has crushed the heart of man- simply to love and be loved for who he truly is.

Max J. Lewy

## Community Nurse

She is a bit eccentric, and a nice-natured lady,
Dreaming of space or time ships,
And goblins with severtyeight different toes,
But, when all is finally done and snipped,
The party line she tows.

At predetermined intervals she visits me, like a woman's monthly woes.
Making sure that the child inside of me, often bleeds and never grows.
"You've had your chance, to burst buds in freedom", so her teacher says.
"This is for your own prudent protection, for the rest of all your days."
It seems to her a wise precaution, to nip the peaks and tuck the lows.
Because it's at an expert's inspection, somebody who much better knows -
Officious guardians of convention, who society's primitive fear allays.
It is for us a most difficult sentence, because ours are not their ways.

Each time she arrives, how I try and I scheme to prove myself pristinely sane.
Yet all she probably sees is that chequered history, the hideous, unrelenting stain.
Her lukewarm purpose melts the ice that I hold to the swollen wound in my head.
It always seems to me that too little and yet at the same time, too much, was said.
That harsh, baseless and unyielding verdict, that blemish against my name -
When she leaves, I am always disappointed: same picture in the same frame.
I do my best to affirm my resolution, how many important things I've read.
Yet afterwards I feel it was pointless, I may as well have just stayed in bed.

She says it's a past of misdirection, for whom a caring judgement bell tolls.
She says its just a matter of chemistry, there's no such things as souls.
She thinks that its a better destiny, the one in which our spirit, drooling, lulls.
She thinks winds can quickly change, there's no telling which way our mind blows.

She is a bit eccentric, and a nice-natured lady,
Dreaming of space or time ships,
And vampires with seventy eight different souls.
But, when all is finally done and snipped,
The party line she's sold.

# Write To Survive

A poet has the luxury to sit back and be himself.
A poet cares little whether he makes it to the shop shelf.
A poet is wise beyond compare.
A poet sees something fair everywhere.

I am not wise, I see nothing fair;
But if I don't prove I'm alright 'up there',
I'll be treated like shit.
I'll lose what mind I still have, what wit.

In my words, I set no stall.
How could I heed the Muses' Call?
Ever since that little medication board,
I resent beauty as something I cannot afford.

I am something more raw, more pure.
I am something more core, more poor.
Adrenaline pumping through my veins,
Brings the most acute quatrains.

Do I write from the heart?
So what if my rhymes only fart?
I don't write some vain pleasure to derive...
I merely write to survive!

Max J. Lewy

# Golden Boy

Hewn on Manchester's hallowed fields,
In the wake of those woebegotten Busby Babes.
Before their illustrious tradition he kneeled,
Like a dolphin playing sagely o'er their ocean graves.

Shooting out from the demos,
Like some blazing starre -
He left the keepers at a loss,
Nestling his freekicks just beneath the bar.

Announcing himself, in the rush of youth,
Letting waste no time.
He looked up, struck it with Truth,
And scored from the half-way line.

Everything he did with an air of ease,
While the crowds' eyes hung on his pixel-perfect passes.
His manager and mentor, Alex Ferguson, he did please,
As the opposition defence was split assunder on crisply-cut grasses.

Inevitably, the accolades and endorsements rang in;
Bringing great riches to this fair and fresh-faced fellow,
And yet he seemed immune to the decadence and sin,
Holding his head high, donating to the unlucky below.

The girls all swooned at his handsome visage,
And, so, like most men he had to splice!
A girl named Victoria led the charge,
With a famous career of her own known as Posh Spice.

Star-struck lovers art they and were,
Heart upon heart, soul upon soul.
Still, even he couldn't help but have an affair -
This was perhaps his only lull.

Except perhaps for his voice so flimsy, shy and weak,
But then he didn't much need to speak.
He let his feet do the talking,
While his wife did the singing.

A generation of boys carved in his image -
Metrosexual males in Armani underwear.
All in all, he did alot of damage,
To the macho man's au naturel debonair.

Things in the dressing room took a turn for the worse,
I'm afraid I can't lie.
Sir Alex had an outburst,
And kicked a boot in his eye!

So off to America he flew,
Furthering the Beckham brand.
Showing "the states", where they don't have a clue,
How to cross a ball in a way that isn't bland.

We must now blow the whistle,
On this "golden boy",
And, not without a sigh,
Say goodbye, with the certainty,
That he gave the masses entertainment guaranteed;
That his gentle soul gave the world Joy.

## Gentility Without Joy

Spider spindling webs quietly through the night,
Keeping his rage well below the surface, safe from sight.
Gentle as a Lioness playing softly with her cubs,
Without fail, he can be counted to avail the sweetest sobs.

Working his plans out in careful, serpentine deliberation,
His own best interests receive their due estimation.
And of those around him he is diligently gathering,
Even of his foes from whom he is constantly hiding.

Yet he feels no joy in his peaceable temperament,
For him it remains but a fairly weak instrument.
What's more, he knows one grim day it will not suffice,
To keep Satan's minions from their cruel device.

His malice, his damnation sunk deep in him only,
His retaliation is but a restriction of the spirit of charity.
Thus idleness is his favoured vice and Achilles Heel,
Before which each day with gnashing of teeth he doth lay.

## Sacred Jungle Of Dreams

Beyond the dull horizon of wakefulness,
Lies a jungle of multifaceted wonders.
I can almost touch her medicinal mystery;
Their plant-like plenitude beckons me.
If only I could penetrate this shallow film;
The pulsing propaganda of daylight hours,
Where lizards languish lazily below the leaves..
And sink deeply down, hidden,
To the wild womb of even-tide's twilight embrace.
The healing dusk of imagination's tribalistic dance,
The refreshing aroma of midnight's herbs and flowers.
The plunging of life's buried root
And the withering of its secret wick-
Amid stars dripping honey-yellow and bright..
A ritual camp-fire flaring, in the moonlight.

Max J. Lewy

## Just More Meds

The police hand-cuff me and sling me in the back on their van.
The van speeds off, I struggle to breathe and they don't give a damn.
Us damned, so-called demented souls have practically no rights-
Though it might seem right, it is however self-defeating to put up a fight.
Battling for air I try to reason with the chimp behind the wheel;
Wheeling around and around like a rat in a cage of steel.
Stealing is still illegal, but kidnapping has become a societal norm.
Normally they all just follow orders like those Troopers-Storm.
The storm through my nerves a tempest swirls, ripping my soul to shreds.
Get lucky I'll have shreddies for breakfast, but mostly just more meds.

## **Unkempt Stars**

It was little past midnight when I awoke,
And by Jove! I would gladly choke
The lousy rat who did rouse me.
The clammy bitterness on the tongue,
My spirit so sadly wrung
From a better world that did enchant me.

Leaping from my chamber like a Lion aft' the foresaid rat,
Caterwauling and catapulted into the Night,
'Neath a sky matted with blood.

No book of Law beneath my arm,
No bastion of morals to soothe and calm,
But the cold merciless frame of Winter.
A little something, it did splinter.

Mean streaks of ice scattered the Valley,
The weeping willows lurched with eerie malevolence.

Then an angel, or a devil, reared its face before me,
Through the myst, upon the dead pond's frozen surface.
On the wind, it whispered: 'Your friends, they will all desert thee;
Your Truth alone, it must suffice'.

'I know that already', I yelled, still seething.
It cooed sorrowfully yet sagely: 'It's too late. You are defeated
where none hath seeing.'

'True...'

Then the face that had so sadly shone turned blue as the moon,
trailed by beams of unkempt stars
Like the bars of a universal song, Or prison window...

## Lobotomized the Beast

Since psychiatry came to me,
I drool like a dog in my dreams.
Since psychiatry came to me,
I drool like a dog,
Even in my dreams.

Since psychiatry caged little old me,
Everything is even worse than it seems.
Since psychiatry was let loose on me,
Everything is just as bad as it seems,
Seems in my dreams.

They talk over me, even in my dreams,
'til I'm nearly bursting at the seems.
There is no use for screams...

Once there was a Christ-force that dwelt within,
Now grown pale and ghostly thin.
The kernel has been cored-out!
But it doesn't matter how we shout...

666/ 888.
The devil, the seducer of the world/
The Word, the prince of his own soul!
They're all the same - They're all gods.

They come from within,
Come over us like lightening,
When once we were men -
Not as concrete beings or voices talking in our ear, as they stupidly,
self-servingly assume;
On our subtler, yet loftier tongues
(We who imbue humanity with its proper dignity, which stretches to
the divine - which, in a sense, is itself man-made or man-killed..)

Such words bespeak impersonal, inner energies, activities
And potentialities -
Just as 'gravity' names an outer energy.
They are psychological principles or archetypes,
Not angels or demons in outward form, descending from the skies
which only we can see!
Why use such loaded terms, you say, such as 'angels on wing'?
Because they have poetic force...
And the spirit longs to sing !

Now we only have another type of electrical intercession to look
forward to.
What use is joyful rhyme against such contingencies?
In their mean eyes, a dance is a mere fit.
Meditation? An aberration..

To those seeking 'help' -
"Get out before you get caught, and lend a hand to those who
weren't so lucky."
For who will help them who need help (to flee) from their 'helpers' ?
Who can even see which way the earth truly revolves here, let alone
alter its agonizing axis?

I am just a toy, the least of creatures - begging, barking for dignity,
Dignity in defeat.
Like their forebearers, the priests and Inquisitors of old:
The shrinks have carved up my saviour for tea,
To be sold.
For the sake of their foolish feast -
A meal of vanity and greed -
They have even lobotomized The Beast.
Theirs is a religion stunted of both notion and emotion,
Its charisma is like a poorly made wax-work dummy,
Gauche and deathly cold, yet smooth in all its juvenile simplicity.
It would make you too into a mannequin,

Max J. Lewy

An exemplary ticklist of outer inconsequentialities to set beside every barren, burning soul.
For they care about only what they see, they see nothing important,
And all they do is smoke and mirrors. They never awoke.
Because,
Wherever there is a soul burning, MOST PEOPLE ONLY SEE THE SMOKE!

Madness: a form of love

## **Tiny Little Pill**

Tiny little pill,
Gods within kill.

Max J. Lewy

# Born Unfurled

How can you smile, and forget me all the while?
If you are so happy why won't you go that extra mile?
Can't you see the emergency number that my eyes dial?

Must your contentment be a shield that shuts out my melancholy?
Can you only feel love for a cute little puppy, called something like "Molly"?
Am I expected to follow suit and just play with my plastic dolly?
Or suck as a pacifier this freezing ice-cold lolly?

The world settled down in its comfy chair too soon,
While I was busy laying prayers on the pale blue moon,
Clasping to my chest some mysterious ancient rune,
Waiting for some distant, guiding star, Heavenly-hewn,
To play me its melody before I change my sad tune.

Wait! Wait! This spinning cog-like world.
Just as my hair, tightly curled, I myself was not born unfurled.

# The Gondolier

This old canal is filled to the brim with my tears,
For once I was a sage, a king..
And now I am a mere gondolier.
Ride with me down the crumbling streets and ruined ramparts
And marvel at the once illustrious, now vacant alley ways of my soul.

The pure face of the water reflects my pained expression
As I await some divine intercession.
But, alas, many folks come to worse ends;
And the world's spinning does not end.
At least I have a lifetime to assess the sweep of my woe,
To watch for signs of it in the undertow,
To drink it in, from the top of my head, to the tip of my toe.
That's more than many men will know,
Who have never fallen from on high,
Into the murky depths where gruesome gods lurk below.

Most men sleep through it while their family jewels
Are slowly stolen by the passing years.

I leer at the young tourist girls as they come by,
My oar will never take them where they long to go.
Truth, the most beautiful maid,
She who's charms never fade,
Will never ascend this baleful bank.
Thus, my spirit, ever-lank,
Filled with thoughts dark and dank,
In this stagnant, oppressive tank,
Will never even know how very low it has SANK.

Max J. Lewy

# Ben

Mild as milk -
Obsidian eyes,
Like soft black stars.
Hair a shining silk;
Bright as the Night which shades us from lies,
With mysteries hid by invisible bars.

I was always a narcisistic Gemini,
Nothing but a cerebral prancer.
But like the divine Rousseau,
You are a custodian crab, not just swift but steady,
Ensconced effortlessly by the Tropic Of Cancer.

Ever since that grave Winter day,
I lean towards your raven Light, in a quiet way.

Haloed by gentility,
May thine Justice keep thee safe.
When each man flies in every direction,
Heading hopelessly for the hills,
Heavy rain pattering hard on earthly sills,
May thine friends bring thee shelter.
For princely politeness flows from thee
As life-sustaining waters to fallow sands from the Nile delta.

May your temperate spirit come to know,
To grow in humble serenity
Towards the empowering grace of Wisdom's almighty bow.
Voice of vibrant suede,
Let your arrows be shot with care.
For life rewards those on the side of truth, not mere dare.
By knowing the phases of the moon, one is able to turn with the tides

And, through subtle manouvres, sometimes even direct their history's loom;
Rather than swimming, like I have tried, always and in vain against their forceful flumes.

Everything I say is but a glimpsed reflection,
An inference based on most feeble powers of detection.
Though I have long been adrift on inclement seas,
*In your youthful image I pray for a better and newer me.*

Max J. Lewy

## Your Apocalypse

Curtains descend... for the end of this small play called History.
We gods sound our applause - some rapturous, some a little bored.
That it had to end in total tragedy was hardly a mystery,
Nothing is sweeter than a heroic failure to the heavenly Lords.

After all, we wouldn't want competition;
Merely to entertain, that was your mission.
Your fate might easily have proved worse;
For you there was no better purpose.

From our seat in the stars, we took in the breadth of your woe,
Your joy and your sorrow, surveying your mortal voyage from afar.

A catastrophe, yes; But a comedy, also.
Creating mischief amongst you made our merriment glow.
Catastrophic tides, scorching Volcanoes,
Earthquakes galore, and oh-so-much more. How we adored
Fabricating and then obliterating your tiny hopes.
Disease, starvation, war - the standard tropes.

They may be cliché, but still amuse us in their way.
Such is only fitting, for mere animate clay.
BOOM! Thus goes your last hurrah; we shout 'Hurray!'.
Didn't you sacrifice enough? Did you forget to pray?
Haha! You poor fools! That was all a ruse, a ploy to add to your dismay.
If we chose for a moment your bitter suffering to allay,
That was but a short delay, just for a passing day.

O, Look how I rhyme and dance with such glee,
Upon all the broken bones of your pathetic misery!
See how I skate upon your empty plate,
And happily mate with entrails of your hapless fate.
So in love, so erotic, and though it may seem so misanthropic...
We are gods, and to us your mortality was something so exotic.

Madness: a form of love

In you we tasted transience as some delicious farmyard dish.
Forgive us if we could not grant your every heart-felt wish.
It would have deprived us of fun had we been that squeamish.

A 'God of love'? That's fair enough. But don't begrudge a little
schadenfreude from those above!

O passing dust, you thought you could become as gods amongst us;
Your technology, with such guts and energy, aimed for the Heavens.
How beautifully ironic that it struck only the abyss.
As for those others who pinned their hopes on Messiahs and 777s-
Those fools we shan't much miss !

Like all good plays, of course it finally ends.
But, all in all, you put on a brave show..so as you take your dying sips:

WE SALUTE YOUR APOCALYPSE!

Max J. Lewy

# Through A Window Paine

The garden flickers from the falling rain,
As I watch silently through a window paine.
Everything in it by Mother carefully arranged,
By tears of the sky today is changed.

A sparrow sits upon a leaftop,
As the cat stalks closer it hops,
And flies away. Just like my luck did
When my wild heart I unhid.

Like rose-bushes, we ourselves must be pruned,
Before we are allowed to blossom and come to bloom.
Sometimes the cutting goes rather too far,
Then it ends in bloody pricks, in stunted men and civil war.

All envy a spirit that is free,
Lesser folk fall down, worshipping thee.
Heaven is Mighty, the Sun is pure;
A savage phase in your offspring, indulgently ignore.

## 'Mad Community', or, A Small Bird Willows On The Branch

Soberly checking his dentistry
for miniature radio transistors,
Dreaming of wild sex, with his royal daimon sisters,
Taking a bite from the moon each night,
To dutifully ensure its sacred cycles
Turn as beautifully as the wheels
Of penny-farthing bicycles.
Our maligned malingering neurotic,
Certainly has a taste for the exotic.

Objectifying, labelling, separating men
And women in to little boxes with surgical precision,
Taking his medicating nails to the rickety fence
Of their brains, and hammering them one by one, in.
The good Dr. prowls from ward to ward,
Butterflying from one hospital to the next on
His highly esteemed, highly important business.

A clash of cultures, I suspect..
Will the esteemed Dr. stop for a moment to reflect?
On the misery of his charges -
Their private world of enchantments -
Nay, nay, he rides over it rampant,
Feeling fortunate he is not among them,
Reviled by his peers for the company he keeps!

A small bird willows on the branch,
Its chicks destroyed by avalanche.
One man's gaze locked within,
Imprisoned by his inner divining mirror,
The other, consumed in the reflection he makes
On the bank statements and collegiates,
Exiled from source of spirit,
And, both equally so, from the ever-healing wellspring
Of true human community.

Max J. Lewy

# Night Stroll

Through the skylights, the moon calls palely down,
Gliding across at its frozen pace, tempting me from my lair.
No coat needed, I slip effortlessly from the paneled door,
Surrendering to the veiled Night's missive, mystic allure.
Clad in checked shirt, I ride the winds down the patio,
To the chip-barked path that traverses flowers, foliage, trees;
Heart still crackling with the ash of previous nocturnes-
A soft piceous breeze ruffling my long cotton sleeves.

Lantern gleaming from across the pond, I wander
Further into Cimmerian shade. Slinking through the dell,
Upon the hill, liaising with firefly and daffodil,
Bargaining with moth and May weather.
Assuring the Azaleas that everything will work out well,
Comforting the Camellias that rain will soon come,
I ramble deep into the garden, with ownmost knell,
Taking a light swig from my flask o' rum.

In the not-too-distance, through the corner of my eye,
I spy a star shaped like a hammer falling to earth,
Above the sickle of a crescent moon. .
An omen, a premonition of a Holy War and Pious Lie;
Can the ways and justice of old sustain us,
Or will they crumble, come June?

I put my mind to my ear, it is a simple shell;
I listen rapt to the strange currents that tarry.
The starry dome, above me like a gigantic blueberry.
The earth beneath my feet, so wholesome and well.
I hum a rhyme, by the old oak tree.
I throw a dime, in the wishing stream.
The old painted barn, it never seems to rust,
But I am rusted now in innermost dream.

# The Day I Gave Up On Mankind

Some say the road to happiness lies in sacrifice to humanity.
On the contrary, only in abandoning it did I find
My own suffice to be free. Only by,

Flooding the house I lived in,
Throwing the bookcases out of the window,
Making light of the cripple...

Only by,

Snipping the throat of daffodil,
Pouring poison into the sea,
Wantonly going abroad ripe with leprosy,

Did I breathe a sigh of sweet relief.

The day I gave up on mankind,
I kicked a pebble into the sea.
Where it went thence... To sink or to skim...
To dash the brains of a seahorse...

Or buttress an underwater Kingdom...

What business was it of me ???

The day I gave up on life,
I drank merrily; I played the harp; I danced the cobra.
I joined a local political organization,
I looked up a jogging group,
I went to Church,
I swayed like a silver Birch,
And fell over and stared up at the sky.

Max J. Lewy

I wondered why, but I didn't half-die over it.
I felt so weightless,
I might just loose grip of this grassy dome
And fall into forever with all the other stars....

Because, you see,
Mankind had damaged me so completely, so thoroughly,
So terribly badly,

I no longer held out the slightest hope
Of teaching it to sing in harmony.

*Madness: a form of love*

# Ode To Lunacy

O you bright, brilliant mesmeric thing,
Why not lift up your voice? Raise your voice and sing!
Here on earth is a place where angels take wing,
And to eternity hymn their wedding vow.

Beneath the glow of incandescent night,
Acronychal cryptic acme of insight! Vagrant's delight!
For us whose eyes are pure there is plenty of light,
Also a good time for tipping a cow.

Let your wild fancies trample across the skies,
Don't let them closet you! With their wherefores and whys,
Such prim impostures bring only sighs,
Forget the formless future, embrace the now.

For there is reason in all things, madness too;
Dionysian frenzy, self-forgetfulness! Purge all fretfulness, undo the blue!
Transcend all boundaries, even rhyme a little ramshackle...
Anywhere the wind blows, here is my tabernacle.

As I sail by each lambent and illustrious star,
I may see you, finally see you discovering who you really are...
Everywhere there is strife, all things at war;
Watch over the turbulent seas, see the moon and softly crow...

A bright, life-shaped bubble of victory begins to glow.

## **Doctors And Madmen**

At first I looked and saw that all the Doctors were failed Madmen. Then, I looked again and saw that all the Madmen were really failed Doctors. That means that the Doctors were really failed, failed Doctors. Two negatives make a plus, so that means they were indeed successful Doctors - presumably with healthy paycheques and good lawyers

*Madness: a form of love*

# City Sage

Shunned by the trance-laden masses,
Spat on by the self-appointed 'elite',
Just around some dirty corner street
In every major city, even today,
In his sleeping bag curled up within
Some dusty back alley passage way...
A Buddha patiently dwells -
Waiting for the world's holy wonder to re-awaken.

\*\*\*

By lying low on crowded streets,
I rise like warm vapours from vents in the pavement,
Above the multitudinous mind.
I have, I am - everything and nothing:
My words shout surrender, but my voice is filled with design;
Without a penny to my name, the entire city is my boudoir.
For them it is a battleground of all against all.
But pity and gratitude are the portion on which I survive;
Hand-outs to my cupped palms put a swagger in my stride!

On many tempestuous nights have I revelled like an awe-struck child,
Frolicking freely through the neon wilderness, or riled.
Greed makes the garbage cans brim bountifully for me,
Yet I exist without the trappings of mainstream materiality.

The moment is forever balanced perfectly within,
And I am at the very centre of the storm-
The mesmerizing mass-market parade -
The hub of it all. All verve through their nerves,
No stall - at every stall.
Inwardly still, inwardly me.
You think I'm the exception?

One of my comrades in alms is Jesus - only with breasts -
And another has tales and tunes that would put Tom Waits to the test.

Max J. Lewy

One look at us, sitting with blankets on the sidewalk, and the coldest hearts melt.
We may not be at home in our beds, but are we not more at home in Die Welt ?
In this free-access condominium beneath the stars,
Love, I take in, multiply and radiate outwards
To the tops of skyscrapers down to the shadowy unconscious sea;
Which we homeless embody as the archetype of this poor suffering humanity:
For - and remember this, ye who build your castles so proud and so tall -
We are all as beggars before the mighty One And All.

Madness: a form of love

## Little Superman

Little superman shies away at school,
Knowing not how his contemporaries to rule.
He keeps his head down, acts dumb, and plays the fool.

Klein Ubermensch frets about his Schuler,
Dutifully arranging his pencil and his ruler,
He doesn't have an outlet for his lactating lunar sadness.

\*\*\*

He thinks about his gladness, how happy he is to be himself.
Because of the cruelty of his classmates, he sees only little demonic elves.
Why waste good time and effort, developing the self ?
In a world of such pettiness, he is already on the top shelf.

There is a poet, a philosopher trapped inside.
The world is not ready, its safer his virtue to hide.
To watch himself decay, through the formative years.
Deaf to the calling of fate, the callow corn has no ears.

"But when I come to think it, do I blame 'Satan's little minions'?
No, no; it wasn't they who restrained my little pinions.
It was those who never taught me to nurture my deepest orisons.
Never to meditate, never to feel, never to enjoy, never to relax;
Never to utilize my desires, and push my abilities to the Max!
Too bogged down with routine and homework,
*To ever become anything more than simple clerk!"*

*Life has no prior meaning, it has to be sovereignly willed.*
*His heart has lost its rudder, but the world will not be stilled.*

*What will be the result, of these piling arrears?-*
*The growing guilt for neglect in so many areas-*
*When he finally gets the bill delivered in the post,*
*'tis mostly malice he entertains the most.*

*Scything through sentiments of success,*

*Giving himself over to rank duress.*
*Berating the bloody-minded sanguinity,*
*That for so long substituted vital spontaneity.*

*A lion roars, but devours*
*only itself. 'tis only April showers.*
*His true untapped powers,*
*Finally arise like triumphant towers.*

*But the old bullies in the playground,*
*Have meanwhile built their own villainous mound.*
*For his residual syncopating sadness,*
*They now call him new names: 'mentally unsound'.*

*Magnifying his ills a hundred fold,*
*With poison pills new and old.*
*Constant surveillance to make sure he never breaks the mould.*
*Or leaves Dr. Frankenstein's faithless feverish fold.*

*Against hearts so empty and cold,*
*What use he has now lit a bulb so beautifully bright and bold ?*

\*\*\*

*Little superman, because he never began to cultivate his soul,*
*Learning badly how over their eyes the wool to pull,*
*Knows not how his contemporaries to rule.*

## **Surreptitious Smile**

The raging circus goes on far below,
'tis a sorry sight, a pigsty of a thousand woes...
But, we are too wise for sorrow
May as well fatten the sows!
This is a land of plenty for those who know.

Our thoughts are the liquor that everyone longs for,
The forbidden fruit that all desire to eat.
But their primitive 'gods' hallow an imperfect Law,
So it takes guile to avoid the Mercy Seat.

That's why our writings are painstakingly labyrinthine.
With soothing myths, we fatten the kine.
With teachings superficial and asinine,
Fitted flawlessly to the mould of the mass mind.

Sometimes we ourselves have to make a cull,
But it doesn't mean we don't care.
Every dog has his day;
An unruly mutt our collective future might annul.

We are the brightest yet most distant stars,
Only those with the keenest eyes can see who we truly are.
Our words and deeds are cloaked in mystery.
If we ever die,
We return to the earth with a surreptitious smile;
The shadows that we leave behind, others call History.

Max J. Lewy

# Vaccine Against Love

Didn't you know too much tolerance allows even tumours to thrive?
Negation, discrimination, exploitation are the upright backbone of life.
Only those with a faulty moral immune system preach Unconditional Love,
Remember: there is more Wisdom in the serpent, than there is in the dove.

Don't make a habit of turning your nose up at Hatred,
It makes a great panacea for mending the heart that charity rends;
With a bit of cunning you two could be successfully mated.
Your Will should be unshakeable, with unwary acceptance it bends;
Be kind to yourself for once, let your righteous anger be sated.

Don't become the victim of all the mindless passing trends;
Stay stalwart, an unswayable rock, amidst the changing winds.

Impose your vision on the slumping clay of other's indecision,
Soon you will see the beauty in the fruits of your own fateful mission.
Then flames shall kindle and ascend from your loins to your brain,
To make sure your countless foes are paralysed, declawed, or slain.

## My Prospective Ubermensch

Studying "The Gay Science" on a public park bench,
When up walked a local lad, my prospective Ubermench!
Thinking him a poor dupe of the doctrine of 'sin',
I decided to unlock the untamed beast within...

"Hark! I teach you the Superman!" -
"Alright, where's your cape?" -
"Not that one, you ignorant ape."
CRASH-WALLOP-BANG.

Phew, that was a close escape...
At least the security camera caught that ruffian on tape!
Good thing he didn't see the book - it could have been rape!

Thus ended my philosophic hunt;
You're lucky around here, if you can catch more than a grunt...

Max J. Lewy

# Beautiful Id

Freud annoyed the drug-barons, by proposing the 'talking cure',
When he spoke of 'healing through love', their jaws just hit the floor.
Still, he didn't eschew their ways completely-kidnapping remained to the fore,
Not wanting all his business to dry up, or to lose test-subjects galore.
He gave the squalid profession an ounce of intellectual allure,
Allowing it to grow beyond the confines of the four padded walls.
Suggesting the hidden sexual motives of humanity, especially of kids,
He did his best to shock - nay, appall -, like all outstanding yids.
And even if, by Joe, his work was mostly titillating fables and fibs,
At least he managed quite well of extreme prudishness the world to rid.
He excelled in showing how society, makes our true natures become hid,
But because of his inherently hypocritical profession, only half-lifted the lid.
The way his heirs rape and pillage their patients, it is an ugly sore,
That leaves all true seekers amongst us, wanting so much more.
We await that liberator of the spirit, to go so much further than he did,
To tear away the straight-jacket, the chemicals, and free that beautiful id.

## **Arising Aurora**

This desk is a cage,
The war that societies wage
Against the free, wild
Mind of the child.

Stack them in a row,
Hush-up their cries of woe,
Their mother will never begin to know,
One day we shall reap the bitter seeds that we sow.
This is how they treat those who have never even known
What it means in blissful light to have grown.
Work their poor little brains to the bone,
Then send them home to moan.
Oh, how they will groan!
These baleful drones...

Then, in the summer holidays, a fair few will get stoned.
And the doors of perception will open...
And the school gates will shatter...
And they'll realize its not the rat-race,
But their own souls that matter.

And then they'll no longer be prisoners, but outcasts.
Autodidacts arrayed with an argent aura of arising aurora!
Like Terence, they'll use their ken, taste the fruit and sample the flora.

## Love's Little Vandal

Love's little vandal
- a pretty criminal, indeed-
Has engraved far the from the driver's station..
In her grotty hinterland
At the back of the bus...
Upon the seats that rust,
Where reluctant riders rest
Their rotund rears...
The holy, miraculous letters
Of her true Love's name.

Just another petty crime,
*Putting the world to shame.*

*Madness: a form of love*

# The Phantom

As a child, fear of ghosts kept me oft awake, yet as in a daze:
It was my mistake, my horrible haze.
(Oh! The errors
Of our terrors...)

As I grew, I tasted the fruit, the courage,
Of a kind snake.

I became the salutary outrage
of eternal light.
I unravelled the finer mysteries
That shrink from sight
And made peace with the night
That had threatened
To keep us ever wettened
And white.

But as we had exited the darkened cave
To claim our birthright, no longer a slave,
A new monster finally gave

Us a reason for our until-then false fright.
And though we fought with all our might
The fiend broke the beautiful, dancing kite
That we had sent out as our emissary into the Light,
And it fell from a lofty peak
Back into the terrible Night!

Now it is fallen apart at the "seems" -
They think they know which way my heart leans
But see only their own troubled dreams
I would wean them from their fusty schemes if I only had the means...

Max J. Lewy

Is there nothing uncanny in this old charade ?
Or will I even keep them up "on-ward"?

If they only knew
The terrors
Of their errors...
They would never sleep soundly again.

Now I am a phantom,
A vaporous myst, obscuring the earth, that wants only to chase
others from their stuporous repose
But, for a moment, I was a kid of considerable ken!

## **Gaudy Grin**

Your radiant eye beams down warmth upon me:
I appreciate the kind invitation of friendship;
And, hungrily, I accept.
But I'm not too hip
With this world, you see -
Our situation leaves little room for sanguinity -
So forgive me if I cannot reciprocate your gaudy grin.
For when the grim Lord rears from his terrible fort in the Royal
College Of Psychiatry,
And all is left undone,
I'll leave it to the mortician's art
To bring a smile to these impregnable lips,
And finally fake a fond farewell, and wedding ring,
To all that is, was and will be.

Max J. Lewy

## Shrinking Between The Lines

Yes, Doctor, I'm doing very well;
Please don't give me those pills,
That send me straight to hell.
*(You are not the man to cure my ills.)*

Yes, Doctor, I'm going out a lot,
Don't put me in one of those rooms,
Where they feed you through a slot.
*(When I come here I smell doom.)*

No, Doctor, I am not 'seeing things',
And, I would never consider praying.
I don't believe in angels on wings,
*(I try not to see anything at all.)*
\*\*\*

Of course, Doctor, you are a man of the mind,
*(You're so sharp you could have diagnosed
Leonardo Da Vinci With ADHD, imagine what
He would have achieved on 'adequate doses'...)*
But \*ahem\* forgive me, Doctor..
*(All you ever do is talk about my boner.)*
All of histories heroes you've yet to find.
*(...Have you even read your Homer ?)*

*((No, I don't mean the people who's testicles you used to electrocute.))*

## Neptune's Daughter

I am Neptune's daughter. I carry
Ancient salty sea in my veins, and all
Its watery wildlife. Daddy is an old git
With beautiful merman scales. He sails
Above the ocean squall while I squat
And watch from the cliff,
Wondering if the jet net and
Hack-harpoon of my heart
Will yet catch a fat whale, or holy haul of
Salmon, sunset pink. Obscured by
Needle-fish violence,
And the jejune juice
Of squid ink.

Max J. Lewy

## In The Garden

They don't twitch a muscle until you're dead,
Until all your gold has turned to lead -
Safely buried, in the garden of Mystery.

In the Womb of Nothingness;
The Tomb of all our Hopes,
Where lost loves forever Bloom:
Obsolete but unsullied,
Unmarked, perfectly intact.

Then they spoil your rest with their weeping,
Their reflexes become activated.

*Madness: a form of love*

# The Lilac Lighthouse

Lilac spectres, hovering above the rollicking waves,
Greet me at night from across the oceans... as I hold
The fort by the old lighthouse, beautiful and bold...
Caressing my mouse-white beard, upon this misty eve.

Like lavender flowers, of pallid hue, they skate upon,
The perfect blue, of the frozen skies... Flooded with white light,
From the bulb in my citadel by the sea. What dreams they carry,
From what storms they are sent, over life-less bodies,

Broken by tempest, shall remain shrouded in night.
But, that they come and go, of this there can be no doubt.
Of the agonizing nights spent alone here, left only to watch
On while so many souls ran aground on the breakers.

*We begin as star fish, and end as empty shell.*

I bore witness with my shining torch, until this day,
When my madness finally sets sail, and I join them...

Throwing myself off the high porch, into the eternal blue...

## The Gravest Sin

I love you truly, madly, deeply.
I want you to be content-
Like a new born lamb, Heaven-sent,
Nursing upon its mother deeply.

You crave pain, because
It reminds you of your childhood.
It must be difficult, being misunderstood;
But I am at a bit of a loss.

Should I regale you in further suffering?
Should I tie a tourniquet around your loins,
And throw the wishing well a few coins?
Is that the compassionate thing?

I love you truly, madly, deeply,
I want you to be content-
Like a new born lamb, Heaven-sent,
Nursing upon its mother deeply.

Your self-doubt, while charming,
May be clouding sun, moon and stars;
But you're shining from the planet Mars.
Lover, your desire is embalming.

It preserves the beast in me,
And nurses the child in you,
On the teat of blackest hue.
Your tears replenish the sea.

I love you truly, madly, deeply,
I want you to be content-
Like a new born lamb, Heaven-sent,
Nursing upon its mother deeply.

Madness: a form of love

Your tears replenish the sea,
Putting paid to your father's grin.
Little girl, accept yourself and be free.
Guilt is the gravest sin.

## Non-Coercive World

'Liberty', your name on every tongue.
Your lips carry the Call of all-along...
From deep within our breast,
Wherein our thoughts do rest...
And percolate in solitude,
Above the teaming multitude...

Exhorting us to become ourselves;
To go deep within- shun the shop shelves...
So that our Being is of our own choice,
So it reverberates in a distinct and clear voice...
So our actions, under our own sure command,
Remain clear of consciences austere reprimand...

'Liberty', let your name not merely be on our tongue,
Or the flag behind the barrels of a thousand guns...
Or the poppies over the fields of Afghanistan,
Or the whalers around the seas of Japan...
Nay: but let each man become his own child,
In a non-coercive world, of mad mercy mild...

## Close To One's Chest

I wanted the glory of my love to be heard,
So I whispered it on the breeze to a nightingale.
But, alas, that dreadful bird,
Turned out to be a goose with a tall tale.

She twittered of my crush,
As if it were not the burning bush,
But merely throwaway, momentary trash.

My pride took an almighty crash,
As I saw my heart's ideal shrunken
To the spectacle of huge, ghastly
Runaway genitals, isolated on legs.

For all the kids kiss without much ken;
They will try to project onto you what is most nasty,
Surrounded by a bubonic racket and beer kegs...

And even in the grown-up world,
Your adoration will be equally slurred.

Thus, I learned to keep my love a secret,
Hidden by cruel gestures and lewd acts.
It is the stuff of black initiation and blood pacts;
Even holy writ is too vulgar, it only serves to cover it.

For the most honor one can do all that is best,
Is to keep it forever close to one's chest.

Max J. Lewy

# Rumination On Self-Assertion

I was once a diligent pupil, had no clue but passed every exam in town.
I felt the twinge of scruple in swallowing all that had been written down.

My brain was just a tin,
Full of garbage they put it.
This magnificent machine
Reduced to something so mean,
So passive, so thin;
They even had me saying,
With an hollow voice, 'Amen'.
I knew not why or wherefore,
No joy or bon vivant,
I was a ghost, lettered tombs my haunt.
As I tried more - greater burdens I bore -
The more I was bored by it all.

Years later, I found myself lazing,
And my soul set to blazing,
In an auto-reflective process
Who's only measure is its own pleasure;
Rumination on self-assertion/
Adoration of its own salvation -
That stimulates and engrosses
In a way that docile, out-ward centred
Obedience never can, and usually censors.

We must all listen to the voice of Nature, of the gods within -
in order to begin our blossoming;
But don't take my word for it - look within!

*Madness: a form of love*

# God is inside

Relax your mind,
Let pleasure unwind.
Find only the whys
That bring you joys.
Permit your environ,
To be your sweet siren.
Search for clues in the surrounding air,
You never know what adventures lay hidden there.
Let your sensations be your vocations,
Let them lead you on long vacations,
'til you find your perfect home.

Don't be afraid of contradiction,
Opposites have a complementary jurisdiction.

Remember to
Savour each second
Like a heady glass of wine,
On a warm, carefree night in early September.
Allow your senses and intellect to intertwine...

Be not the mind's pale minion-
Live every moment, each has its own opinion.
Let your taste-buds tingle you towards the Truth...

There's no hurry,
But if you like, you can let things come out in a flurry...
Or, patiently, one step at a time.
Be silent; mime.
Breath deeply, and count to nine.
Refresh your feeling for nature's wordless design.
Let your Will sound out like the valiant voice of victory at the vanguard
of a thousand armies, like a long-going gong of glory!

Max J. Lewy

Try to stay balanced snugly at the centre of your own orbit,
Or push yourself to extremes until you feel the definite urge to return.
Send out your tendrils until you touch the seams of the psyche...

Live dangerously!
Don't try to predict the consequences of your actions,
It may detract from the joy of discovery.
Don't demand the answers up front,
Have faith, and you'll catch them on the hunt.
Don't think; just inhale and pray.
Let your nostrils nestle, proud and primal, on your high-browed prey.

Finally, let great plans swim back into your ken,
Not like a surly, unobtainable wench, but like a long-forgotten friend.
Let the lambent stars light up and link your lonely pilgrimage...

For, whatever, "come what may"-
God is deep inside you - this is The Way!

## Courting Fiasco

Pretty and nubile,
This sporting young lady -
Skips gracefully around the court.
Loose, lithe, limpid limbs
Dance and swing, easily in the
Surrounding, sweetly scented air.
Her brow knits seriously
As if interrogating a potential lover,
The bouncing ball impends.
Then she whacks a winner
Straight down the line,
Effortlessly past me.

## The Death Of A Flower Girl

"If hope hath flown away in a dream or in none, is it therefore the less GONE?"

I met you in a Church garden, my crude-crafted polygonal character
crashing into your lovely high-definition pre-rendered flower-bed.
You tended me like one of your daffodils
Healing me with one of your white magic spells.
I knew from that first moment
That our love would be all too brief.
But little did I know that you would be stolen away
Long before the slick end sequence...
Sweet heroine, with footsteps so soft you hopped into my heart,
I wasn't ready for any love but yours.
Why, oh why, Sephiroth - you, who I otherwise loved also as a character -
did you have to cut her down ? From that day forth, everything in my life
turned black...
How I searched the internet, hoping to undo
The fateful work of that terrible blade,
Hopelessly cheated and betrayed by fake promises of resurrection...
Aeris- your name still hangs on my lips, ringing with tears and regrets my
childish recollection.

## Madness: a form of love

Madness is a form of love
It comes from up above
It is wilder than the rose
And gentler than the dove

Madness is a form of love
It carries its own unique truth
It lets the old forget their grief
And makes messiahs of the youth

Madness is a form of love
It longs only to be recognised
Though you try hard not to believe
Or look through another's eyes

..So many years, so many lies..
..Your society is simply overly-sanitized..

Max J. Lewy

## On The Notion Of 'Effort' As A Virtue For Life

A small child is banging his head against a brick wall.
The wise father watches on, his formidable brow locked
Into a deep frown. After a long, irritated silence,
In which nothing could be heard but the banging of a child's
Head against a wall, The reverent man finally exclaims:
'You're never going to succeed like that. You have to bang
Your head alot harder against that wall if you want to find out
What's on the other side!' Meanwhile, a cat who had been
Preening himself lazily in the sunshine, eyes the couple warily,
And then slinks nonchalantly around the side of the wall.

## Aurora Borealis

A light beacon in the iciest of regions,
Solar winds full of both brilliance and bluster-
Glory of trenchant travelers from afar;
Skyward sorcery that time does not mar.
Shining with such a wonderful lustre,
Lantern of lucidity wherefore philosophers seek a Reason.

As every Winter grows thick,
The prowl of the sabretooth,
The hunger of the polar bear,
The pale of the moon's watchful eye-

When one begins to sigh,
Wondering how your frost-bitten fingers will fare,
Knowing not how to go on, in sooth:
Suddenly, into place your bones and thoughts begin to click

As you look up and see her,
Fluorescing ever more wildly, frantically bright-
Shimmering blue and silver-
Fiercely haloing over you through the Night.

Her loyalists curse the cold which she can scarcely resist,
Trekking miles to reach her through the Evergreen forests.

She has the heart of a snow lioness
Looking after her cubs through harsh distress.

But though her beneficiaries honour her in a climate that's chilly,
She is not really averse to the comforts of Man.
In fact, she is a Lady of both magnanimity and indulgence
That it is yet unwise to deem too silly,
For she glows beyond all treats to a greater span:
Appearing before earth with a gift of utmost refulgence.

Existing by herself, like a hummingbird on a higher plane,
Where memories ancestral are stirred up, that have long been lain;

Max J. Lewy

She unfurls and recharges in proud hermitage:
Ready to awaken, in you, in loneliest season and age.

Ready to ignite, when all hope seems lost;
Ready to find the Will to survive at any cost;
Ready to make the shoots push up even through the frost.
Ready to bring warmth and nourishment like the perfect host.

Though she is not perfect this much is true;
To the vulgar, her vanity sometimes stoops to kowtow.
Too in love with the humble creatures she ensnares, with a 'wow', and a 'woah'...
Too in love with the image which the crowds drew... So enthralled to the show...
Hiding from her own lofty view
Her faults - covered by too blinding a virtue.

Mother, I still love you.

*Madness: a form of love*

# O grim Lord, why art thou so blue?

O grim Lord, why art thou so sombre, so serious, so blue?
Death comes to everybody, even the very few.
You have the honour to harp-sung heroes meet,
Who will all one day fall down flat at your feet.

Doesn't it fill your heart with pride?
To cut down such great men in their prime.
And other lesser souls, who have often sighed,
At being cheated of even a dime.
Must you not be glad to end their misery?
And bring a curtain to the mean horizon of what little they see.

Birth is agony, life is woe;
What more is there, else to know ?
In the "fields of rape" our souls are sown,
Into what portion am I henceforth blown ?

Of course I am only kidding in what I say,
Haven't you heard of the man named Aubrey De Grey ?
You should enjoy it while you can, you see,
The day is coming when Man shall achieve Immortality.

O grim Lord, I know why thou art so sombre, so serious, so blue.
Death comes to everybody - even to you too!

Max J. Lewy

# You Live On

A rose grows and blooms, it struggles through harsh soil
Reaching upwards towards the light of the sun.
A stag cantors through a gushing stream nearby,
The flowery, unmistakable scent filling his nostrils.
The stag sips at the pellucid waters, stopping for a moment
To listen to the sound of bullfinches chirping,
And watch the heron swoop down and catch a salmon in its beak.
Then he shimmies on, the remembrance of this moment
Lingering forever, until a couple of months later when
A ruddy-cheeked hunter in a bearskin jacket
Fires a bullet through his chest, penetrating his heart.

You were my one true love, and now you're gone.
But I'm happy, because, like that rose, you live on.
And though my own heart has been pierced, so do I.
We are both part of the same universe, the same society,
And I know you are out there making it sing.

## **Penning Poems**

Penning poems for posterity,
Heroically, I bounded down the bus
Without pausing to look back
And reflect
Upon the seat
From which I flew
So impetuously
At what I left -
My gloves.

Captive of my own levity,
Drunk on intellectuality,
Full of flippant sincerity,
Whipped from behind by reality.

My fingers don't feel a thing,
Until my heart floods them again.

Max J. Lewy

# Dionysus On The Dole

I wear a masquerade ball mask,
And am trailed by melancholy nymphs.
Well, bi-polar single mums, that is!

I ride the South wind down the town,
Leaving mayhem in my wake.
The coppers are easy to ditch,
They're hardly awake! Or on the take!

For those who have not the strength to conquer, their only hope lies in surrender!

\*\*\*

Wine flows freely on my lips;
We come in gulps, never sips.
Breaking the balustrade by life's river,
Making sure they all fall in.
Ecstasy, silence, pandemonium and sin.

I am the fateful diver -
Morose machismo,
Law-shattering lethargy,
Insidious inflame -

A spur of destruction and rebirth;
(And that's just this cut-throat economy!)
Collecting my welfare checks of course...

I am a god, I don't need a job.

I bring madness, I bring joy.
I stir you into incensed rage like a toy.
Why am I not hunched? Why am I so elated?
Why do I have the nerve to lay low and yet resist unabated?

Madness: a form of love

Give in, give in, to my Mesmer-eyes-zing;

We all end up in the gutter eventually,
But only some of us ever truly rise through the pipes!

You think I'd work for 8 bucks an hour?
Yeah, well, maybe... but I'd rather your souls devour!

I give the shrinks the cold shoulder;
Sure of an insanity plea, I just grow bolder!

Ah yes! My disciples and I are crazy orgasms incarnated...

Tremble, oh ye weak-hearted.

Max J. Lewy

## Beneath The Bell Jar

"The Nothing noths" about me,
My world muted by innocuous jar.
Try to search world beyond me,
I am blocked by invisible wall.

The actress sings fine melody -
Her lonesome call cannot reach,
The numb charade of merriment,
My decorous portrait bleached.

'Daddy, won't you wish me luck?'
'Daddy, aren't you there?'
You, the brute in boots of black,
You, with scowling, unseeing stare.

I always thought I would fly,
Like the Cuckoo in the air.
But now I've decided to say 'goodbye',
By disappearing to nowhere.

Madness: a form of love

## All Quiet On The Frontal Lobes

A battle was fought: his Medulla oblongata versus an electrical socket.
The electrical appliance distributors made a racket. So did his screams.
But its pure, scientifically certified - who am I to besmirch and mock it ?
From now on his ol' rumbustious spirit won't be harbouring queer memes.
It'll be pliant, malleable, ductile. The vibrant brio, fizz of magnetic emotion,
Will have dissipated with the deafening circuit of cerebral electrocution.
They'll be no more fuss, no mayhem from his once truculent warrior soul;
The trenches are filled with the fallen, but walking graves no longer howl.

Max J. Lewy

# Psychiatric Scapegoat

The priests in white coats are carving up another offering,
Your son, your daughter - send them to us for offing.
Once in our hands, they will be dead long before they're in their coffin.

A slow, tormented sacrifice is our new-fangled device.
So long drawn-out, unnoticeable, with a treatment that's chimerical,
We can all pretend we're doing them good with this cruel chemical,
And just lock-up all Kafkas whose axes might shatter our ocean ice.

Or why not re-introduce one of our old favourites,
One which can turn men into mice with but one slice?
Lobotomize the wise, rescue them from fate's roll of the dice,
By fulfilling their worst nightmares all at once.

After all, destiny can't rob them when they have nothing left.
So turn a sage into a dunce. After their spirit has lost its heft,
They'll be easier for both of us to control. Let your consciences lull.

Have no fear: if they continue to talk back - ohhh, the temerity! -
We'll follow it up with some electro-convulsive therapy!

If there's one thing we can't stand its talk of 'the soul'.
In our view, men are genetically-programmed machines,
Tiny cogs who are simply no use to us when they're on "the dole".
We resent it very much when a good slave asks what it all means.

Let's all pretend the notion that virtue is developed is a myth.
That poetry and philosophy are just some sacred shibboleth.
There is something inveterately wrong with your own kith -
If they throw you a sad, betrayed look, just plead the Fifth!

Sweeter to believe than that their was some fault in their education,

Your own sins for which you now seek this perverse and awful oblation.
As we rob another life of its savour, for the slightest anomalous behaviour,
Drugging your kids until their brains are no bigger than a hen's,
The cheque in our wallets, the fake lump in our gullets, shall be our "amen"s.
So, please, submit this to your most penetrating lens.

Would you like us to operate, or have you still left some decency and common-sense?

Max J. Lewy

# The Voice Of A Babe

In Sicily, a château on a hill stands silent and still,
Perambulating spirits hath here lain hid,
No corporeal vessels vaulting their lingering will,
'Til newly weds appear with their infant kid.

From the shadows, something leaks and speaks,
In the voice of a babe, quoting ancient bards.
The cobwebs won't wash off, the floorboard creaks,
A child's swing fluctuates loose outside in the yard.

"Hateful to me as the gates of Hades is the man
Who hides one thing in his heart and speaks another"
So the little one did sagely and queerly chant,
To the marvelling murmurs of his young mother.

In days of yonder had she wild liaisons spent,
The lustre of love which could now shine for no other.
It was no use, her soul was a thousand ways rent,
The husband caught the clue and left her for another.

*Madness: a form of love*

# Picked

My grandfather was a diamond miner, down in North Africa.
One day deep at work in those dismal caves,
His bronze brown skin baptised by the hot, heavy, teary sweat,
That bled like a refreshing, summer rain from mid-day's labour,
A fellow miner's pick flew free from his grip;
It became a mad dervish, spiralling effortlessly,
With fate's terrible weight and necessity
Backwards towards my poor grandfather.
It's iron claw punctured him straight through the heart.

If our lives were like perfect flowers, poking upward through the brown soil of eternity, we too would have, by now, been picked.

## Sunrise, unrise!

I prayed for mountains,
That I might climb.
I prayed for sunrises,
That you would discern.

My merit to prove,
Your love to alight.

Then the world spun on.

Night by dawn,
Down was torn.

Stars fleeing, flickered out.

My might too bright;
Your wood, too thick.

*Madness: a form of love*

# Silenced Song

Silenced song.
Where is the one I have loved all along ?
Without a sound,
Never to be found,
Down in the ground...

(They all shout) Turn that face to a cheery grin,
Or else you're in for some electrocutin'.

The Triumph Of The Will? Nil!
Killed by a pill.
Yet Herr Hitler haunts us still,
In the minds of those who label others 'mentally ill'.

I'm sorry if to you my words sound awfully shrill;
But this here is no trifle.

...Feeling 'ill'?

No hesitation: Straight to the Concentration Camp!
His blinding white coat? His cowardly armour, his priestly cloth, his
Jew-skin lamp.
Turn you to a slug with his drug, then they stamp on you still.
So merrily he smothers the lives of others, festooned by his adoring
peers as they watch on...
So happy to be a 'scientist', so happy doing wrong!

He knows that he's 'successful',
(Although it's all a con),
He knows that he's 'professional' -
The common herd just go along !

(They all shout) Turn that face to a slobbering grin,
Or else you're in for some electrocutin'.

Max J. Lewy

Silenced song.
Where is the one I have dreamt of all along?
The rain falls
As it has done all along
But is no longer redolent
Of arcane memory - of teaming life, and Siren's sweet Song.

Words vibrate in the ear, but not in the heart...
Words vibrate in the ear, but not in the heart...
Those bastards nipped my bud at the start.

Psychiatry: Like a mortician's art.

(They all shout) Turn your face to a gaudy grin,
Or else you're in for some electrocutin'.

Madness: a form of love

# Brain Is Broken

Brain is broken,
At least give a small token,
The moment I was awoken,
Was precisely the moment it was broken...

Living with disease, degeneration,
Became my permanent occupation.
This is what becomes of those
Receiving 'mental health services' attention;
Induct you into a ceremony of ritual degradation,
Tell you this is your whole life's Station,
Put you on toxic medication,
Self-fulfilling its own prophesy of invalidation,
Producing chronic deterioration,
Sending the bill to the nation!

But once, in ways that still require some adumbration,
In ways that escape those fools powers of concentration -
In fact, being sadly beyond ALL demonstration...
This is why I am now hell-bent fury of frustration...
appearing of 'madness' incarnation! -
Being unable to prove the cause of reparation
And achieve a modicum of just restoration -
But once, I assure you, I was the budding architect
Of my own soul's infinitely precious salvation!

Brain is broken,
At least give a small token,
The moment I was awoken,
Was precisely the moment I was broken...

Hark! When one is in a state of psychic perturbation,
Of intense inner concentration, she requires the most
Exceptional care and compassionate consideration...to give

birth to the next spiritual generation....her own personal Christification...so next time, save this 'blitzcare' obliteration and abomination operation or once more sentence your own innocent child to an agonizing, life-long damnation, hearing, hearing, and once again hearing its pitiful excruciating lamentation!

## Sullen Sun

A dash of light between the clouds,
Behind them a raging spite.
I never thought this day would come to pass.
Now, I look on it bleached-white.

I look on it like the maple leaves,
I look on it like the Flood,
The seven Scythes of serpent's Hill,
My palace has turned to mud.

I watch from the old Canyon,
Into which I did fall,
The funereal high-flying march,
Softly tolls the Wedding Bell.

The bell in all its macabre,
The bell in all its spite,
Says that I married to none;
Alas! My only heart,
Was the poor wife whom I did fight.

I have not seen the sun rise,
I have only watched it set,
All my diamonds fell to pieces,
This sullen sun shines yet.

And when in trance I wonder,
Who made this misery veil?
I fall short into a thunder,
And struggle to lightly exhale.

Max J. Lewy

But once in yonder grove,
An apple tree did climb;
The not-so-sullen sun shined down,
Ripening fruit o' mine.

Ah, this is a foul, unknowing beast,
Of whose schemes this world is set.
This sullen sun has fall'n from grace;
His apple was a fool's bet.

Crushed to cider dust,
The sickly colour of our light.
Vainglorious and indolent,
And cannot repay its debt.

Sullen with malice,
Sullen to the hinge,
No apple lurks upon this tree:
Sullen sun-dreams of revenge.

## Mad Transgressions (Put Acid in the Pope's Woopie-cushion!)

Predictability, sanitization, lethargy, routine.
Humdrum, normalization, resignation - obscene.
Euphemism, everday-ism, truism...

*What else can these mean?*

Colloquialism, rationalism, blandism,
Conformism, scientism, hypocrisism:
Mental morphine!

Sheepism on amphetamine.

How it all, how it all provokes...
How it all provokes: my spleen!

It is really all, much too much, to even be seen,
By the many whose eyes are covered by - a dream.

'O how adult, oh how sedate' -
(Such is the way, they hide their hate!)
'I am frightened of death, I am frightened of life;
I think I'll just keep my head down and stick with my wife!'

I have a plan, I have a scheme:
To free their minds of this sterilization team.
\*\*\*
A dangling crucifix... a bloody roar!
We hope to make the soul a little less obscure...

Dance free in the meadow of perplexity!
This life is one of contradiction and complexity -
You have to be a bit strange to make it through all the adversity.
So: don't stint now on a little 'perversity',

**Bataille on steroids is hardly enough!**
**Think 'Philosophy in the Boudoir' — we like it rough!**

Our startling claims and acts will reveal it
in its Being - Such to almost justify the timid in fleeing!
Something bold, something knuckle white -
Something to amaze and lighten up the World's Night -

Opening it to presencing,
Disclosing its true nature,
While covering it in confetti;
(Do you enjoy the biscuits, called 'amoretti'?)

The unconscious is wild, release your inner child.

The world is a stage,
And on this, my page,
I intend to wage,
A war upon the mediocre.
(*You! Yes you*! I'm going to put a sprinkle of LSD in your tapioca!)

Put acid in the Pope's woo-pie-cushion,
And laugh it off.
*Yes, you queer, I am a toff!*

Because...

Reason is a dreadful bore,
And madness, sweet madness:
Madness is more honest, more secure,
More alive, lubricious - more mature -
More pure, more core;
Enough to make you soar;
Something, *most definitely* **to adore!**

# The Failure Of The Enlightenment For Man's Moral Education

Just like the microscope, modern day science as a whole, in many ways, makes the world in which we live a lot uglier. In its fanatical fight against "illusion" at any cost, its Promethean bid to infiltrate to the hidden causes of all things, it has forgotten the humanly essential phenomena itself and robbed Life of the natural perspectives which render it worthwhile. When it attempts to address these phenomena at all, i.e. in the form of psychiatry, it has turned into a mere parody of itself, utilizing the jargon of science and its claims to universality, merely to sacralise unthinking and vulgar societal norms. Meanwhile, it teaches that Facts and Values are irreducible to one another, effectively rendering (at least for those under the sway of this absurd theory) the natural arbiter, which is Reason, impotent when it comes to deciding upon practical courses of action, and giving intellectual (i.e. the highest) license to absolutely anything - which in practice usually means whatever most other people are doing, but also includes the most stupid and heinous crimes imaginable. It has thus abnegated its duty to cultivate our souls through the sweet allure and enchantments of poetry combined with the noble, careful exposition of philosophy, towards the True, The Beautiful, The Just. In its materialist myopia, its mono-mania for what is universally perceptible and reducible to numerically verified Laws, i.e. the outward physical world, it not only draws our attention away from our lived experience, (which is only truly revealed to the bearer), co-opting the mental apparatus for issues foreign to its real needs and desires, but often denies the very ontological reality of our own inward life (for instance, in the case of Behaviourism). Again, the inevitable result is self-alienation and shallow conformism. In Sum: what was originally intended to be the liberation of Man has been turned into an ideal ideology for the production of unreflective cookie-cutter slaves. Today's religion, i.e. 'Science', is anti-life in a more radical sense than the desert dogmas ever were.

Max J. Lewy

# The Morgue

Nestled near the back, in the basement of this colossal, degenerate hotel,
Lies the neatly stacked, chilled remains of those who are no longer ill.
The decaying remnants of those whom even the blade could not save,
Whose tortured spirits, on disinfected tables, gave their last breath away.
No manner of modern tinkering could out-do their incurable fate,
Now they lay in a man-made limbo, lingering on, yet lifeless, they wait..
Rather like they did while still alive on all those sundry, gargantuan lists,
As the rain and wind ripped all the roses to shreds, through the rising mists.

All you geriatric gymnasts, leaping from one death-defying illness to another,
Your tricks will come to an end here, just like your incontinent old mother.
Those who never amounted to much in life grow in stature in this place.
They have been through a lot.. probably even more than you or I...

Botched jobs, tumorous children, murder-victims...
All gather here together, coagulating like a muddy river in stormy weather.
For the next few cold hours, the buzzing florescent light will be their only hymns.

Surgeons sleepy from too many long nights on shift....
Their heroic failures line these corridors. Throw another Martini into the mix,
Its time to drown our sorrows. Not a few of these quiet inmates were killed by cocktails of their own....Pharmaceuticals is big business, after all.
But the real errors, like me, still walk amongst you. Proud, ashamed. Not nearly so tall...

## My Struggle: The Triumph Of The (W)ill

It's a little known fact that old Adolf
was turned insane by a psychiatrist.
The same nefarious profession taught me that,
in this world, the only person you can truly rely on is yourself.
As Charlie Manson said sagely once, when asked to give a word of advice
to his illegitimate children who he'd never met,
*'You've got to make it on your own, kid.'*

## Zeus Beware

Merrily, merrily! We celebrate your doom.
Nothing is more enchanting than a human tomb!
Except, perhaps, a tomb of the Gods!
Their ghastly corpses linger on in our absent noses
As fragrant and sweet as a pocket full of posies !
Millennia of your longings lay buried beneath the sod.

Skeleton bones clatter on coffins like xylophones!!!

Frolicsome! Frolicsome! We waltz around your graves.
As pleasant to us a rotting saint, as a galley full of knaves.
La, la, la, la, la, la, la, la, la, la, so the music swirls.
The guest of honour - a buzzing, blue-eyed fly,
Beholds it all! Like a panoramic camera's looming eye,
Deep into the night the festivity whirls.

The dolphins are throwing themselves into the nets,
The prodigies are pumping themselves full of pills.

Harken to my words! My bygone beauties,
The world's end is nigh, and, I, Hades,
Shall finally rule as Lord over this pitiful planet.
Such is the wisdom that Time knows,
With each new epitaph, my army grows.

## **Even Paper**

Like the silver birch shaking its trunk
Autistically, in front of darkening grey skies,
How I yearn and pine to be able
To my tangled thoughts finally untie.
Forever grasping, casting out my mind,
I did not heed the fateful sign,
As the strangled stars were struggling,
Beyond gnarled, trembling branches to align.

In unforseen typhoons calamity struck,
Forcing my tendrils to come unstuck.
Such pain, such woe I did thence brook -
To no avail, as destiny offward snuck.

The root did wither, the stars did wane. All that's left is a frightful stain.
Now we await the falling rain, as we are already neck-deep in the mud;
Standing here, forlorn, might as well be made into wood - or even paper.

Max J. Lewy

# A Good-Natured Malignancy

*"I love the great despisers for they are the great adorers."*, F. W. Nietzsche

The commandment 'Love Thy Neighbour' hangs around our necks
Turning the conscientious into weak-willed nervous wrecks:

In profoundest solitude, I rekindled my heart's yearning;
And laughed long and hard about my former spurning.
Within its alchemical canteen, the spirit set to dining.
How glad I was! To have the luxury of freely maligning
Those proletariats who had kept me for so very long
From finding a corner of the universe in which I belong.
No sooner had the thoughts alighted in my happy brain,
Than my sentiments turned to adoration, from disdain.

In self-confinement my soul took flight;
Spread its wings, soared through the night.
All my secret thoughts, free to alight.
My own path opening up in giddy delight.

To have the excess of strength to embrace
Even the damned souls of my own demented race.

*Madness: a form of love*

## **Birthday Barometer**

Congrats! It's the anniversary of your birth;
A time to weigh up what its all been worth.
A day to measure the pain against the joy,
To pass judgement on your father's potent portentous pride,
On your mother's contented, surrendering sigh.

To inflict such a hazard, can it ever be justified?
Is it not a sin to perpetuate this fallen world?
Could it be expected, a tree from time immemorial be denied?

So many wars and walls between the spirit and its being unfurled:
A fathomless fling of fate
Into which, on a merciless matrimonial knot,
Or just one bawdy blind date- an errant sperm-shot-
One can be so heedlessly hurled.

The lure of life is great,
The final verdict up for debate.

When it exists..
O, how it glitters and dances, always maddeningly just out of reach !
And how bitterly it calls out to us, through Time's tearful mysts..

How to live it, nobody will teach !
Sometimes the uncertainty makes you want to slit your wrists..
Thus, the truth you must search!

Only then must you take out the scales,
When lies acuminate into light, and illusion pales.
Only may you then find, even if the reading is still partly blind,
That the meter is *for the moment* kind-
Never knowing what final fatal warrant destiny has signed...

HAPPY BIRTHDAY!!!!!!!!!!!!!!

# You

You are not what they tell you,
You don't have to be what they say you are.
Everything that has happened to you,
Needn't confine you behind iron bars.
Is freedom really so frightening?
Few in this world are free, fewer true,
(There's a reason why this earth looks so Blue),
But they are not you.
Just take a few small steps, and you will rise above it all.
Rebel, rebel! - be what you want to be.
You will be sky blue, you will be brand new.
You can be a vision of glory, a beacon in the dark;
(Leaping like a kangaroo, or happy as a lark!)
There are countless millions in need of just *one* that is true.
Many are open-armed and ready to receive you,
Lots of new friends their unique chemistry waiting to imbue.
You owe them nothing, but you owe yourself everything.
Now you cannot walk, but once you do,
Soon you will be flying.

Madness: a form of love

## The Turin Horse

Leaden longings lay around my heart,
Long-lacerated horse, broken cart.
Nietzsche's mad, sorrowful lunatic arms
Thrown around me...
My morbid, sentimental charms.
My consolation, my dearest sympathy.

Once a proud yea-sayer, now become a woebegone neigh-sayer.

So fatigued from years of fruitless frenzied toil -
Left only with dilapidated, barren soil.
Where hatred still smokes, though fire no longer burns -
All the detritus of a life that's gone to spoil,

And no great, joyous self-propelled wheel of the mind ever again will turn.

Max J. Lewy

# Medusa's Uncle

Medusa's Uncle glimpsed her once,
When the sun was far from view.
Then she stood stock-still for months,
Her visage turned to a greyer hue.

She was the fairest maid he ever saw,
Her eyes glowed lilac in the moonlight.
But the ancient man was such a bore
She fell asleep for an Eternity's night.

Now a couple of restaurateurs keep
Her in their garden. Gone are the gleams
Of her eyes, but no patrons do weep
Tucking merrily into their sea-breams.

She has stood stone-still for millennia,
But all her loved ones have long ago died.
Those who pass praise her youthful air,
Medusa's Uncle is the only one who cried.

He cried for her, and he cried for others,
Whom his stare had frozen forever in tracks.
His glance so terrible, it petrified his mother,
And anyone not sensibly turning their backs.

He wanted only to love them, was it a crime ?
But instead his gaze killed her. In sooth,
I am the artist, who beheld her curt youth.
The veracity is fatal in these eyes of mine.

*Madness: a form of love*

## Britain Finally Gets Up Off Her Knees

They called us the 'R' word, they called us stupid.
With many sneers and much froth, they accused us of being haters.
They tried to bully us into choosing slavery.
They thought we'd sell our very soul
For a few pennies, cheap holidays and Bratwurst.
They thought we had grown so fat and complacent,
That we'd let the barbarians invade without raising a finger.

They thought we'd let supercilious would-be tyrants
Gently rape us.

THEY THOUGHT WRONG

With great dignity and steel, we rise up.
With great tenacity and zeal, we will soar.
They wanted us to decapitate ourselves,
To surrender the head of the political body,
Unable to make our own laws or decide our own destiny.
They wanted to turn us into a suicide bomber,
Voluntarily blowing ourselves up on a 'higher' call.

They wanted their kleptocracy to dictate how
We live our lives in matters great and small.

THEY FAILED

With great dignity, with steel, we rise up.
Digging in our heels, the others will follow our lead.
Germany, France, Sweden,
Spain, Greece, Poland,
Holland and Denmark,
and all the other great nations; break free -
And join us in a FREE, DEMOCRATIC union

Defending little girls and OUR MINDS from circumcision,
Upholding our common, civilized values and humanity!

WE RISE UP

Max J. Lewy

# The Only Race

Liberal education for all.
Machines pulling night shifts.
The mending of our rifts,
Nobody just 'another brick in the wall'.

Joy in pure Being, spreading like syphilis.
Sexual liberation, pure animal exaltation!

Disease the relics of the former pharmacratic era,
When many patented drugs brought profits nearer.
Rejuvenation, gene and stem cell therapy, freely
available and enforced on none. Civil liberties won!

Everyone standing proud and tall, vigilant of
the sacred rights that tyrants once abhorred.
Born free, and living with serene equanimity,
Free to unfurl as we would have our souls be!

A citizenry who can tell, the morally depraved from the well.
And without executions or drugs, bid their sorry ways farewell!

No longer merely 'she', or 'he', but hermaphroditic gods,
Philosophers of the future, partaking of every genre,
Every culture, every race, every creed, every gender,
Who are able to imagine themselves in all types of company!

Star-struck heroes of virtual worlds or teleporting through space,
Military-industrial complex decayed through luxury and abundance.
No need to kill or enslave each other, we've recognized it's redundance.
No longer against each other, but just to one's Higher Self, the only race!

A brand new humanity come into its own,
Breathing a big relieved exhalation, still feverish with creation!

Competition for giving, glory to the philanthropist -
He who on his solitary voyages will be most missed.
He who is most radiant, whose gifts shine like the sun,
Not he who is most rapacious, and lives in an emotional slum.

## Creepy Conscience

It takes courage to be a creep,
To be different, and seep through enmity
Without letting out a peep. It takes goods
To keep it all under your hood, while
The women wail and yelp at the littlest blip,
Or one drop of authentic human blood.

I know that you want to sleep,
And pretend -It's O.K.,
I will play along with your charade.
You're so tired from all that wailing,
You deserve a rest. Close your eyelids.
Send your kids to old grandad.
It's better that way. What's hid
Won't bother you until another day.

Furtively; stalwart - I will work towards a better world,
In the silence of Night where Dreams become unfurled.
When too many tears make your painful vision blurred,
My creepy conscience is round-and-round again stirred.

Save your gratitude for 'God'.
In me your secret prayers,
The ones that you're too afraid to voice,
Are always heard.

## 3/22: The Seeding

Air is crisp
and full of light,
petals begin to pounce
from their
cocoons,
ladyboys leap and flutter.

Brooks babble, smoky exhaust pipes
Create a miniature green-house effect,
Magnifying the sun's warmth,
Holding its rays captive.

See the farmers planting our GMO,
The roar of engines never wanes,
Speeding from place to place.
Everything is re-set in motion.

Chemicals in streams and pills in their blood streams,
Snooper's charter securely in place.

'Top secret' human experimentation,
Mk-ultra and Guatemala Project?
Check!

But. more is necessary,
On pristine days like these,
to keep evil still ablaze.

What we sow now with the knife,
We shall reap in joy, order through chaos.

Madness: a form of love

# End In Fire

Once there was a boy who played the lyre
And swore allegiance to the funeral pyre.
So many mad hopes his brain did sire,
Because he knew it'd finally end in fire.

He worshiped the war-god of Ares,
Letting great flames roar among the trees.
Around them he fabricated a tribalistic dance,
The force of his fiery muse to enhance.

He dreamed of a song of all the world's desire,
To lift him into the Heavens and from the mire.
For years and years he never did begin to tire,
Because he thought it'd finally end in fire.

How dearly he pined for the things to come,
But never at the expense of letting a moment run
Through his grasp to the wet graves below,
Without fanning the flames, as wise winds blow.

After writing his winning tune, a band he did hire,
An orchestra formed of instruments made of wire.
He nicknamed his group 'The Hell's Friars",
Because he said it'd finally end in fire.

Some folks remember, some folks forget,
This was a life the boy never would regret.
Because he knew that it was but a passing berth,
He made the best of all his time on earth.

He rose to riches, sporting elegant attire,
But married a prostitute, a wench for hire,
Their love was as hot as a blazing funeral pyre,
Because he wished it'd finally end in fire.

Then one night, by the conflagratory hearth,
In the haze of love's delirious aftermath,
She said from their union she must demure,
Having re-hooked up with an ex-customer!

But even when things grew really dire,
He never became a baby, a little crier,
His genius, it flatly refused to expire,
Because he remembered it'd finally end in fire.

Still, for his undimmed passion they finally
Donned him mad. How sadly, how blindly
This world accuses those with strong ideals.
Filling the gaudy public press, the camera reeled,

With myths of his final entendre.
They say he built a bomb with bits of wire.
But they are all rank and pitiful liars,
Because he was resigned it'd finally end in fire.

The truth is much more terrible, much worse,
And hangs like a curse on every nurse.
The doctors names are coated with shame,
It is their quackery that is to blame:

As the electro-convulsive treatment grew nearer,
His body combusted from fear with a charge nuclear,
Immolating a good half of beautiful, flammable Gaia.
It came as no surprise to him, it couldn't have been wryer :

Smoke covered the earth, but his spirit soared higher;
Because, as he had predicted all along, it finally ended in fire!

## Teenage Trends

I just heard of something, strange and new;
I know I'm exceptional, could this be the clue?
Now I can externalize, my sense of alienation;
I'll just quickly engage in, a bit self genital-mutilation!

Am I a boy, that's meant to be a girl?
Am I a girl, that's meant to be a boy?
Straight to clinic, no time to unfurl;
They're making money, my nature destroy.

So conflicted in my social identity,
So in thrall to the group,
My body is its carvery,
I'll become its poor dupe.
At least this way I'll fit in,
With the hip crowd be in.
My fleshly temple in the bin;
No offspring for me.

God, forgive me, I was still too young to realize that this was my only life;
Daubed in medical paraphernalia, from the day I was born;
Too innocent to comprehend the irreversible evil of that surgical knife.

Created whole, but now I am torn.

Max J. Lewy

## **Professional Licences**

Nightmare in the air,
A little death in every breath.
I hope to sleep tonight;
Better yet today.
And dream my demons away.

If only I could sleep,
And never wake up.
Never wake up to the consequences
Of passed inadvertencies.

To a spiteful, unforgiving world,
Whose very love is made of poison.
Winter is in our hearts,
In your eyes lies no reason.

My tongue has been removed,
Now I emit only wails and
Tortured silences.
I am a slave to those
With professional licences.

*Madness: a form of love*

# The Infowarrior

Through the long grasses, a lone villager spies;
He takes a deep breath, crosses himself, then opens up his eyes.
He is sick and tired of believing in the ubiquitous lies.

A chorus of voices keep shouting him down,
Begging him not to look, casting a disapproving frown.
But a small, inner call is stronger than them all.

So he steadies himself, and takes the plunge.
Through the castle gates, out of the dungeon.
His spirit begins to lift and his heart begins to surge.

What does he see, not a caring lake of wellness?
Not a concert of kindness, but a sly symphony of callousness.
A secret festival of death and deceptiveness.

The air is brisker here, chemtrails some way behind.
Wind whipped by wisdom, water still tastes of fluoride.
Many innocent corpses lying down by the roadside.

Vicious vaccines, child-sacrifice, cancer-causing GMO rice;
Self-inflicted wounds, secret human experimentation, turning men into mice.
Fascist, pseudo-liberals creating a Prison Planet, putting Freedom on ice!

What can he do, against this Machiavellian scheme?
Either lie low... or go out and spread this meme...
And turn this worldwide Nightmare back into the 'American Dream'!

Max J. Lewy

## **Stockholm Syndrome**

She follows her prescriptions to the letter,
Safe in the knowledge that they know better.
Perked-up by the placebo effect,
Garnered from those in authority.
They tower so tall, over her are so erect;
So easy: surrendering to the will of the majority.

They probe and they prick,
With sessions so slick,
Yet so invasive.
Because its so pervasive,
So easy, to just go along,
To sing sadly from the sheet of their hypocrite song!

'Oh I am poorly! Oh treat me, please!'
'Treat me, daddy! Treat me daddy!'

Rather than have her voice loudly drowned out
By those white-coated gentleman
She dare not live without-
Only to be roughed around by their idiotic henchman.

It would too deeply wound her vanity
To admit its all just a sad masquerade.
Just one giant profanity,
Just one big charade.

After all, she just craves a bit of attention.
Foolish woman, you are the bulwark of convention.

Madness: a form of love

# Piloting The Soul

When I was just a toddler,
I started *wrestling* the controls from my father.
Now, all by myself, I'm spinning 360 degree rolls!
I'm sailing through blue skies, I'm soaring in thin air.
There's nothing to catch me if I fall,
So I must heed the radar.

I must keep monitoring the wind speed,-
The barometer of social nicety -
I must avoid collision with other planes.
I must keep one eye on the passengers - my urges -
To make sure their exquisite balance remains.

The earth is my theatre, my panoramic view.
My picture book, my museum,
My nature reserve, my zoo.
The options are almost infinite,
But I must keep dead set of my course.
The map book, I binned it,
We're guided by The Force.

Why do we keep flying? Why do we not cease?
I cannot close my eyes, I cannot know release;
All these tiny dots of men,
So small its beyond my ken!
To the fields of rape we call history...
It is one big unwieldy mystery.

Oh! They're all blowing hot air, I'd be better off in a balloon!
But the spirit is set on ascension; we're flying to the moon...

Max J. Lewy

# The Moon In June

In Summer of Youth I turned my face,
To gaze upon the world by a plentiful place.
Where the moon shines gay until dawn,
And thoughts by its still, tranquil eye are born.

Since time immemorial, she has done her duty,
Sanctifying the skies with her solemn beauty.
She never shirks or skives, only coyly hides-
This graceful princess, Ruler of the Tides.

As the vendors stack away their ice cream cones,
Her pallid light glitters somewhere on ivory bones.
Passively, she highlights the heat like a silver kite,
Setting the souls of lovers everywhere alight.

Wine flows freely on their subtle, supple lips,
As she chaperones the swaying of their hips.
Through tropical branches she vividly glows,
Blending a little joy with all strife and woes.

Though she herself is barren,
The folk beneath make like hares.
Forgoing the safety of the warren.
And fornicating amidst approving stares.

The air is soft, the breeze warm,
Wicked delights are free from harm.
No gaudy sun to strike alarm,
A priest on hand to cast a charm.

Until she tires of her forceful grip,
Of this earth on her monthly trip,
Her peaceful face will never fade,
O'er the sea, above the forest and the glade.

Madness: a form of love

While nights are long, storms are fierce,
Wine is heady, and songs do pierce,
She always hangs there above serene,
To teach us what our destinies mean.

I would that mine were ever righteous and fair,
To act in Truth, not mere decision or dare.
She promises me the Wisdom of the unconscious -
'Lunatic' is the name of my sacred conscience!

## **Blueberry Bodhisattva**

Calling out his inner God,
With heaps of mackerel pate and big platters of cod.
Fresh, fastidious, fatty acid Omega 3,
Feeds our brains for the visions we see!
Blueberries and soya milk,
Devoured by those of our ilk.
Our Matcha green tea ceremony,
More sacred than Holy Matrimony.

Behold, the dietician!

Stringent fasts are such fun.
Getting acquainted with our own vulnerable materiality,
Knowing ourselves down to the bowels, down to the guts,
Brings greater ecstasy than the emptiest of rituals,
Or the kinkiest of sluts!

Nutrition is my religion.
When I eat, I feel God move in me.
I touch and transcend my own mortality,
For another day, if not for eternity.

THIS IS TRUE MEDITATION

# Madness Is Everything!

Sanity is a small box,
Beware those who tell you what is 'normal';
Its just an excuse for non-thinking herd mentality,
Conformity to everyday evil.

Madness, unpredictability is the necessary revolt
Against the stultifying tyrannical 'powers that be',
Without it we shall all perish ignominiously.

Madness is everything,
The essence of thought - an over-turning without aim -
Authenticity, pure joyous outrage at worldwide complacency.
Dirgeful melancholy at self-righteous castrating stupidity.

Restless fire without end.
Life, conscious of itself at last,
Glorying in its own eternal cycle of destruction and rebirth.

Let your will say: the madman is the meaning of the earth!
Will to power and nothing but,
Will get us out of this dismal rut.

Max J. Lewy

## Hearing From History

Save your paltry prayers for one who cares,
I'll be the one pushing them off the stairs!
You could spend all night embellishing me with your tears.
At the beginning of the new day,
You'll still find me marring your precious careers,
With the jeers of one who cheers not for the gainful 'nears',
But the faraway suns.

The ones which flare and die,
Not in the instant of your debauched sigh,
But under the aspect of eternal jubilee
Do forever rise.

You say 'that's just' me,
In your fetid, faithless eye its all a matter of relativity,
But wait and see,
What goes around comes around:
Get off your settee and join the ranks of the free
Or you'll be hearing from History!

## Care Plan Is A Cruel Plan

To kill in a fit of rage,
Or hot temper,
Is one thing.
To punctiliously plot it out,
In a carefully woven charade of do-goodery,
Making sure every little brain cell dies
According to the rules,
Week by week, day by day, hour by hour,
Is a whole other, far graver matter.

Such a cruel care plan
Contains
A truly *enviable* malice.

Max J. Lewy

# Bon Appetite

Consider man's modern-day best friend, the household hound, compared to the ancient shaggy-haired, silver-crested, Prince of The Night. What a terrible fall from grace this once-proud beast has suffered. Millennia of dependency and dilapidation depriving him of the beauty of the wild. And what of Man himself? Has he not undergone a similar doleful transformation?

The lion in him has been reduced likewise to a domesticated cat. Alas! The sun has truly set for him, reduced to a mere flash light.

O! To see him laze at last freely along the Savannah,
Or duelling bravely with a younger male specimen,
Or mating openly with the proud lioness.

O! For him to stalk his prey through a snow-laden forest,
Or leading a pack of his fellows through the night
Or howling in abandon at the moon.

Do such manifestations still exist? Perhaps.
Just not on the farmyard where I was raised,
Where the poor, fat deluded animals loudly
And hatefully decry the precious sweet breath of freedom,
As if it were a bane to be apprehended on the double,
Rather than a blessing to make hearts wobble.

As Nietzsche said, their creative act is most definitely a 'No!' Unfortunately, I realized this too late. Got too filled with hate. So... Particularly for a Knower, I also remain much of a 'No-er'!

I am but a barnyard pig, thoroughly spit roasted
With a (forbidden) apple in his mouth.

*Madness: a form of love*

# The Neon Isle of Inner City

I will arise and go now, and go to the inner city,
And a large skyscraper scale, of tar and metal made;
Nine accountants will I have there, a hive for the worker-bee;
And live alone in my flat, well-paid.

And I shall have some peace there, for peace comes fleeing ennui -
Fleeing, - quick!- the veiled morning to where the typewriter sings;
There midnight's all a simmer, and noon a man-strewn sea,
And evening full of up-to-the-minute things.

I will arise and go now, for always January or May,
I see neon light flashing with fleet hue by the sill;
While I lay prostrate by the door, or lost beneath the Birch's sway,
I see it in every maddening daffodil!

Max J. Lewy

# Save a care and don't help, don't even help the helpers

You want to help,
But only on your terms.

You feel obliged to invalidate my unusual opinions,
To look askance at my world-view.

Can kindness be mixed with so much disrespect?
You're a yellow-belly, Mr., your anathemas should be more direct.
I don't want your pity, when you treat me like shit.
Come on, be a man: round us all up and gas me, just like your predecessors did it.

Either value my mind or leave me alone.
I am not your pet, I am not your dog.
No man is built to have his very sense of reality derided.
Do you still think we're unter-mensch, half animal?
Of course you do.

Let's be honest: you wheedle and trick your way
Into the ways of men for base profit.
At heart you're a cold-blooded, intolerant monster.
You don't care about me, what good is a charge you don't rate?
Do you get weepy now and then at the thought of our poor plight?
Yeah right! (Though you might act it)
You're just too money-grasping to say 'no'.
And you don't even have the decency to admit it....
Possibly even to yourself: now that's frightening!

If you ever do feel an ounce of genuine sympathy,
It is only because of your own base, animal nature,
Which you project onto poor unfortunates like me.
And, no doubt, it is only for a moment;
We can be damn sure you never let it conflict with your 'duties'.

### Madness: a form of love

You're preying upon the best instincts of humanity,
To nurture and care; And turning them into the worst instincts
Of humanity, to control and subdue.
Let the families deal with their own mess,
And see if they have the stomach to do what you do.

Or whether their better natures shine through.

Max J. Lewy

# Hurled

Hurled into this world - made to muddle through -
Then deluded and hemmed in by social expectations,
Beguiling as a mother's kiss, threatening as a father's fist,
Limiting your identity, and with it, your potential,
In ways you didn't choose.

A nagging sense that something has gone awry,
That there are issues to attend to which others only deny -
Your death, your caged finitude, known but unattended.
An un-willed past and present that needs to be embraced,
Time slipping away..

Locked-up thoughts and ambitions, not yet unfurled.
Habits which bind us daily deeper into a narrow cave.
Plans set in motion that are not our own.
Decisions, decisions, that need to be made.

The dizzying freedom of a world without God.
No ethical absolutes; left to find meaning
In the meager leftovers of the Real.

## **Lunar Portal**

Upon a distant planet, stratosphere long since vanished,
Blue florescent light floats, gleaming amid the ruins,
Scarlet foliage, of some unknown, alien variegation,
Growing up along their ancient walls,
Within which our strange race one dwelt.
A passage way of peerless pitch,
Yawns open as night beneath a marble mantle.
Take a leap, into the wild weird:
Madness beckons, a cosmos of untold beauty,
Secret portal to new, fathomless destiny,
Hewn of Sphinx-like mystery,
Awaiting thine footsteps since time immemorial.
Calling to the intrepid explorer,
Archaeologist of a long forgotten, past life
Stirred only by deja vu.

Max J. Lewy

## The Wheels of Samsara

I was once given a bicycle.
It meant the world to me.
To possess its symmetrical steely perfection;
Skidding down the city streets at full pelt,
Come rain or sunshine.

I dreamt that one day I would ride far, far away,
Over the horizon, to a whole new world that lay in wait.
It seemed as if my entire life was building up
To just that day, and everything until then
Would just be grey clouds in a bitter sky.

But, that day never came.
The bicycle was smashed into pieces
By on-coming traffic.
From then on, I had to make do with a wheelchair.
Now I spend my days racing snails
Down the garden path.

# Gus

Long ago, when I was but a young pup,
Our family feline frolicked in the fields,
Across the hills of our ancient land,
When he happened upon a local lad,

Brushing affectionately against his shin.
The yob held the Tommy down;
Setting his air-rifle in position,
Fired a pellet up an unoffending nostril.

The cat found his way back somehow,
But, alas, he was a broken beast -
A mocking relic of his former self,
Cursed to live on in outward form alone.

The sad episode relieved me of my
Naive trust and hardened my heart
Towards my fellow humans. I learnt
An important lesson, but poor Gus

Just became incapable of learning
Anything, or functioning at all without
Extreme difficulty. To see him gingerly,
Joylessly at his bowl was pitiful.

The vet said because he was still eating,
He wasn't suffering. But it felt so wrong,
Seeing him in that state, we had him
Put to rest. I deserve the same option.

Max J. Lewy

# Midnight Misgivings

Today I woke at 9pm.
At breakfast, I prayed the night away.
I am tired of being awake all day,
But must I hold this sarabande instead?

A grey moon hovers
With its patriarchal inquest -
Like the face of an owl
Or grandfather clock.

I sense the nullity of my efforts;
I cleave only for coma that cannot come.
Rhyme rescue me from
Time's strict invigilator.

Je capitule, Je capitule.

I stare hesitantly at the blank page,
Nothing for company but my empty rage.
Words appear and thoughts dissipate,
Like lemmings heading swiftly for the exit.

# Anthem For Drugged Youth

What, unpassable pills for those who die as chattel?
Only the monstrous laughter of the guards.
Only the deaf docs poisonous prattle
Can patter about their cramped wards.
But mockeries now for them; no Vitamin B checks,
Nor any voice of dawning save the choirs, -
The shrill, demented choirs of wailing lunatics;
And sirens calling for them above police tires.
What kindness may be granted to heal them all?
Not by the hands of Shamans, but by these henchmen,
Shall be done things we hardly dare mention.
Their naive trust in society has been their downfall;
Their flowers the grist on which its machine grinds,
And each slow dusk, a snuffing out of minds.

Max J. Lewy

# Crimson Sails

A local boy came into his inheritance,
And, by Golly, it was no threepence.
He splashed it on a ship, the 'Crimson Sails'.
Hoping to cut a dash on the open tides.
But, I'm sorry, his dreams were denied;
It was soon eaten up by big Blue Whales.

The young lad had lost his swagger,
He took to the streets as a beggar,
But he gained a remarkable ability;
His hands cupped real high in yearning,
His heart began to set to learning-
A healthy new-found dose of humility.

He finally took to it like a fish to the sea;
Deemed a lunatic.. but in that day they were free!
Because he was poor, he was thought 'below'.
But he couldn't care a less. He strove
To repay the coined kindness in Love,
He beamed on all men like a rainbow.

## Sturdy Stalwart Stance

I stand still and silent.
All around me, the world is still too violent.
There is so much to lament.

Who will not accuse me if they see me reflect,
Upon the life they have made for me, so misery pecked.

What evil do I conceal?
How far might I go against the Tao?
Isn't to truly *think* to risk it all?

If they see me turning my back on them,
If they see me turning my gaze to its inner rim
Won't they chase me with raised pitchforks?
Won't they burn me like Guy Fawkes ?

To become something I'm not already,
Based upon a moment of chance;

To finally become something I *am*
Based on a sturdy stalwart stance.

\*\*\*

So many worries, I had overcome;
Then the doctors cocked their gun...
Setting my mind back fully asleep,
For another, agonzing decade deep...

\*\*\*

Stop in your tracks, and you are deemed crazy;
By all around you, unconscious and lazy.

Max J. Lewy

# The Tryst

Her skin so pale, her lips so pink none could resist.
Heartsong long gone, mislayed by years of myst.
Bridal veil, a pall, throwing more darkness over it all;
Could hardly dim out the grave's comely call.

A song so sad and sweet, untouched by human hands-
So she could take flight at last, a bird in distant lands.
Swooning her towards her end, scythe of crescent moon;
To the only place wounds might mend- pray it be soon.

Her husband, so worried, called a speeding ambulance;
A frightful misjudgement of comtemporary circumstance.
But, thankfully, she was *alive* to his thoughtless deeds;
She had a hidden secret store of bitter poppy seeds.

Her skin so pale, her lips so pink noone could resist.
She made a final pact, the ultimate unswerving tryst.
Sharp needle, a tear, after neatly combing her hair;
She settled her account with life and left its meagre lair.

# Meeting With The Most Beautiful Angel

Knock, knock, knock!

"Hello?"

"Its Satan! I've come for your soul."
He points to the blue box in his hand. "Just slip it in here."

I decide to lend the guy an ear.

First he put on a show,
Of his opalescent visage,
His tongue eloquent beyond earthly understanding,
His she-devils seductive and maddening.

"I promise you earthly happiness-
Your ego will be walled up within the bounds of my religion forever,
Rendered docile and content, you will see nothing but skies blue as this box
With nothing to lament."

I thought to myself "This is tempting; freedom is wasted on me nowadays anyway.
But, then again, eternity is a long time to be without a soul; I cannot consent."

Then I asked him whether he was not afraid of reprisals from on high;
He merely tilted his hat and nodded goodbye.

And so he disappeared again, and I did sigh and almost did cry.

Such a remarkable fellow... rarely has come my way.

Max J. Lewy

# Penance

Beyond my
stunted imagination,
lay myriad maps, kaleidoscopic lights,
and enchanted secrets
fit for the most rapt delectation:
carousel rides that last through the night,
circulating the stars - and planets,
from Saturn through to Mars.

I can sense them so clearly,
I can feel them in my bones,
but there is an infinite ocean between us;
thus arise my tortured moans.

Though I try, and try, and try again,
I can never reach the once effortless stem,
snapped by a contorted, misspent youth.

I must spend the rest of my life
filling a beach from scratch
one grain of sand at a time,
Which was once pristine,
Lovely and complete.

Watching the waves, even then,
make mincemeat of my work.
For as far as I can see,
In this world -all future hence -
This is my penance.

# Visions Of My Funeral

I returned to earth for but an hour, to see how the people, they would salute me.
But their displays of sadness and of mournful affection seemed... very dilute to me.
It was but a slight gathering, and the eulogist, missing nary a stride as he walked
To the front of the - I don't say 'crowd' - the few who had appeared there to offer
Their respects, who soon sat down again in their pews, leaning back as if on a sofa.
Squeamishly avoiding my countless hates, passing over all of my inflicted sorrows, he talked
Fondly of some polite, mild-mannered eccentric who had a close relationship with Mother.
The meagre assembly listened sedately, before singing a quiet psalm to one another,
The almighty stench of death pushed back behind closed, soft, pre-fabricated curtains
For another day, another month, another year, where it could fade away once again
Or grow to massive, outlandish proportions, unchecked by the redemptive beginings of sincere and resolute openness that I myself had never developed for certain.

The last thing I noticed before being called back down to Hell, was the uncanny smile
A particularly enthusiastic mortician had concocted on my once- while alive- sombre lips.
I realized then the complete annihilation not only of my physical, but of my spiritual Being,
So that I was only too glad to return to the fiery pit where at least torture is recognized

For what it is.

Max J. Lewy

## Sure Sailing

Everyone is losing their heads and blaming it on you.
Time is spinning by without forming into an orderly queue.
You're humiliated countless times by those you hoped to woo.
You have just learned to wish your sad old days 'Adieu!'

'Friends' are spinning by with sabres drawn at your throat.
You say, 'O.K., I've had enough. I think I'll get my coat'.
You run a hundred miles, quoting the philosophers by rote.
You leave all the meddlers behind on the sourest note.

Cities are spinning about you in myriad shades of gold.
You feel a new-found freedom, at once both young and old.
The Winter doesn't faze you, you do not even feel the cold.
You have escaped the petrifying prison of the narrow fold.

Dreams are spinning about now pulsing with reddened blood.
Finally you feel that your soul is no longer misunderstood.
You see the future brightly, imagining all that there could be.
Deliriously sober, marvellously sane: fuming at all the doddery!

Finally you come to rest, somewhere deep within your chest.
You decide to try your best just to fit in and not be a pest.
Don't rock the boat too much, don't make too many waves lest
The plodders catch onto you. But now, as for me?

I'm riding every crest.

## S.S., Smiley Squadron

Hide away all your tears,
Or we'll cut out your fucking tongues!
The dread day is coming soon:
When 'ecstasy' is required of your lungs.

Like Barack Obama at Trump's inauguration,
Make sure you grin from ear to ear.
Don't let anybody see that you're not content,
Remember: unhappiness is treason.

Don't let the world see that you're perturbed,
That you have dreams, only mere schemes.
Embrace the Now, march to the step of History,
Grin slobbering at your television screens.

A dawn of a new era, a new tyranny:
The greatest symbol of which,
Is not the Jackboot,
But the Simper.

Like Hilary Clinton, mad, plastic eyes and drawn-back jowls:

Obsequious, triumphalist,
Know-it-all paper-thin grin,
Sheepish smile,
Like a shark's fin;
Jutting above the hidden tide,
Jaws open wide,
Ready to devour
Your last reticent cower,
Ready to deny
Your last authentic sigh.

Now we have pills for all your ills,
So you better make sure another tear never ever spills.
Because *we care*.

Max J. Lewy

# Beauty Of The Word

The moon is nigh,
So up I fly,
Passed stratosphere, towards star,
For the place the angels are.

Gracefully, I glide
Across the firmament
Of starry tide
In my silky raiment.

'tis a sea made of dreams,
Where that which guides me, also softly streams,
Under my paddling, feather-light oar,
And, of course, the crescent-moon boat on which I soar.

Quasars, space dust, singularity,
Black holes, comets, and little old me.
From galaxy to galaxy, I am careening.
Long left behind, the **Milkyway**...
The universe is brimming, teaming
With togetherness and sweet equanimity.

Call me a witch, if that's what you think;
Though its unfair, I still won't sink.

I have become a heady bird,
Up above the reaches of sin,
And all that I see, outside and within,
Reflects the beauty of the Word.

## Crest Of Sorrow

Crests of sorrow break upon the silent mid-winter dusk,
Through air light as gossamer feathers, thin and scentless.
The muted revolver of regrets fires a blistering bullet,
Through the mind of this pasty, and stunted, insomniac.
Soundless his head falls, sinking upon the lonely pillow;
Dreaming of baleful doom clouds o'er a weeping memory.
Death is in that gruesome wave - in its gulf, a fitting funeral
For him whose myriad schemes remained so rank unreal.
His virtue, dead as an Elephant's tusk mounted upon some
Rich pharmaceutical executive's hearty living room wall.

Max J. Lewy

# Common Enemy

Humanity: constantly breaking into mutually antagonistic groups.
Thirsting for conquest, fuelled with anger; marshalling the troops.
It seems citizens need a common enemy before they can fully love.
As if there's more wisdom in the serpent, than there is in the dove.
So let cruelty, let misery be our Common Enemy. Fight with great
Might, against whatever plight assails the souls of any crew mate
Aboard this common voyage, torn by the fiendish talons of fate.

There is always work to be done,
Yet you wage war from boredom.
Can you not see,
That there is a greater foe than the one across the sea?

Is your lot so destitute, void and null
That you would stoop to kill
For a greater share
Of the horrified world that's watching out-there?

Think of the sadness of your lovers,
Mothers, sisters, and brothers;
The mess of distress, or quagmire of desire
That craves the sweet song of the lyre,

Or the right words to bring back an honest smile to faded
Eyes. Isn't that something for which you'd sooner puncture a lung ?
Eternal vigilance is the price we pay for freedom, so if you want to
Put your courage to the test, get off your sofa and do some reading.

Because one day, even without throwing your life pointlessly away,
The grave will come to stay. And on that dying day you may pray,
That you'd put down the gun, and just laughed, and said 'Hey!!!!'.

*Madness: a form of love*

# Hymn To The Medicated Messiah

Pure air, shining sunlight,
A conscience crystal-clear,
Reflecting a soul so white,
As the electrodes draw near.

A compact bullet of spirit,
Of bold and blistering merit,
To cut through Night's fog,
And slay the army of Magog.

O, valiant hero from beyond
Lead us to the Elysium Fields,
With a wisdom unfeigned,
And strength that never yields.

Sink not to glib compromise,
But with wild penetrating eyes,
Let forth your insane rage
Upon this unsuspecting age.

O great lunatic, O mad sage,
Write a glittering new page!

Max J. Lewy

## All I Can Really Manage

I play Football Manager.
It may not seem like a noble pursuit,
Watching my pixels run around all day in their little boots-
But its all I can really manage.

My dreams melted before they were set,
Faded not quite into the back of the net.

Raced into distant starry eventide,
And were quickly called offside.

My will has surged and been halted;
Nothing anymore seems able to be altered.

\*\*\*

Like an ointment borrowing bubbles
Of oblivion from the abyss,

A trivial and mind- numbing task
Bringing utterly pointless and shallow,
Yet unfailing, success in which I bask.

Judge me not for this,
Your "Law" has reduced me to such rubble.

\*\*\*

The generated sound of each kick of the ball,
The dull thud of "victory",
The dull thud of a chequered history,
A dull thud to appal.

That has yet comforted me through the years;
Soothing my battered, sensitive ears-
A techno-tissue of constant entertainment,
To soak up the bitter tears of discernment.
Lulling to sedation my hopes and fears-
Since nothing else kinder ever appears.

\*\*\*

Friends, forgive me for spending so much time on this silly game;
As if I were really disabled, degenerate or lame... because now I am.
Trust me, I was not always averse to climbing mountains or lifting
the same. God damn, its not me - its psychiatry which is to blame.
So please your glances of admonition at them do aim.

You can't imagine all the misery I overcame to get even this far.

Max J. Lewy

# Cacophonous Coffin

If I somehow inveigled myself into a position
Of power upon this infamous planet,
I would crush this sinful mankind into dust,
Down to hell would it plummet.
Reconciliation for all the crimes committed
Against the poor child in me,
Would see these earthlings burn indeed,
Until all rank Eternity.

For what is it to be King of the present,
He who has already been cast out by the past?
I seek not to reign over this earth,
But to be delivered anew, a rebirth.
All that breathes and beats I do resent,
From a butterflies wings to Welsh accents.
Who shall bring me the demise I crave at last?

Who yet can destroy me?
Alas, no one but I.
Unhappy, the man his fellows cannot erase.

By the destruction I create,
I am testing the Almighty:.

(O ye God, strike down this weary tyrant!)

Each throat I am permitted to slit is another nail,
Another note in the cacophonous coffin
Of the poor child in me.

# Dreams

Today I felt aggrieved with my lot.
When I took in the span of my plot,
It seemed so mean, and bereft.
All the potatoes were blighted.
As for the grapes, there were none left.
What a melancholy scene
In all my mirrors, all rear-sighted.
Impassable decades of decay between
Me and my true love.

But when I reflected on the grand sweep of History,
The fate of the common man, and Kings on their thrones,
Dwelling deeper on the mystery of the full story -
In a world where most are reduced to brute, back-breaking labour,
And the 'lucky few' listen for assassins' footsteps passed the twlight hours-
It seemed impious of me to send out more moans.

It is surely the destiny of mankind to be miserable.
Masses swept away by lotteries and pop idol contests, oh-so-risible,
Swim eagerly into the awaiting jaws of a shark.
Stirring up their own avarice, prostrating themselves before popularity.
Rather than weeping for the camera and laughable applause,
They should feel grateful for their already relatively comfortable lives.
After all, fame without style is merely a handicap.

I realized that only today does failure seem a fault,
When the loser is blamed for not mining his God-given vault.
I realized that overall my lot was not really so bad,
Although I never felt much pleasure in anything I ever had.
I realized that just today does agony appear the exception,
And in recognizing this I found consolation.
My envy was subdued, my guilt dissipated.

Max J. Lewy

Now I listen carefully for the funeral bells,
In all bright smiles, consumer articles, and wishing-wells,
Knowing they will never lead to Utopia.
If I lose all consciousness and pulse,
Until which day... essential vestiges of my mind and shell...
Can still barely waltz,
No matter what other dreams have turned to Hell,
I'll consider it a Cornucopia!

## Wholly Marginal

After years of inattention,
The cause of sufferings not worth a mention,
I began to read about the Spirit,
And my mind's lever started to turn.
Finally finding the scent,
The outer world it did spurn;
Surviving purely on its own merit,
Inwardly chasing itself, it went.

A journey of discovery,
An addict of misery in recovery.
Waking in midday,
Waking in dreams.

Guided by revelation of the unconscious,
Guided by the light of consciousness,
Experimentation in the alchemical laboratory of the soul.
Abhorring all marginalization, a quest to become Whole.

A search for meaning, a search for perspective.
A voyage drawn-on by instinct:
Nothing shall invade this sacred precinct.
But, lacking the power to secure this environ-protective.

When you go deep inside, the world's jaws open wide.
So, make sure you know how to hide,
Before you go mining for forgotten gold.
But, please, don't let it ly down there forever unnoticed;
It doesn't multiply unattended, like dust, as you grow old.
It unfolds before the sun, gradually, like the lotus;
But it retracts on exposure to the peering ignorance of other stars.
Its element is Venus or Mercury, rarely Mars.

Max J. Lewy

                Paying heed only to the five senses,
          I over-looked the dangers of vulgar pretenses.
             So, 'insane!': this was my cruel sentence.
I advised you to look inside, but now I must keep one eye out!
With these fiends, it doesn't matter how you scream and shout.
     What I needed were mentors, what I got were monsters.
       Now, for shame, I know what to think of 'authority'.
           I have become a small endangered minority,
Fearfully seeking the shelter of my fellow sisters and brothers.

## Small Truculences

A lorry roars by with cold, reasonless anger,
Unmitigated by the possibility of reform,
Of amelioration without destruction.

A metaphor for the ceaseless war.
Each night I ask my mirror on the wall,
Who's the most broken of us all?

Cold wintry cauldron of death,
Disintegration - desist! -
Humility without abject imbecility,
Lift the mysts of our minds
Beyond the trivia of the times,
Toward the eternal themes
That might inform us.
Spring, March to a new step!
Strides of sublime rhymes
And opalescent candour,
Unsullied by piercing crimes
Committed against us
From higher powers.

Max J. Lewy

## **Privilege And Iniquity**

I drink privilege, I breath iniquity.
Everything around me wreaks of docile obsequisy.
I was a born a prince, of a minor province.
And ever since, I have often heard words minced,
By those below, who dare but tow
The line of those above who hardly know
What ghastly sacrifices
Line their perfect patios.

For I was once one of the elect,
But now I am derelict.
But I yet carry the residue of favour,
Even though I am now considered a mere ranting raver.
My heart is broken but my bank-balance is booming,
So I cannot scream without drawing entombing
Glances, which look askance at what I can possibly mean.
There is no punishment for those who have stolen but a dream.

Truly, I would be content in a tent,
But I have rubies to pay my rent.

I can feel your envy already,
Try as I might to appeal to your pity.
Even worse than my wealth, I am in fantastic outward health,
And still even sometimes passably witty.
Yes, one could even say I have a talent,
For constructing rhyme, with sense still all but paramount.

But neither, I suspect, will you feel admiration,
For one whose losses heap up such desolation.
I am thought mad by all accounts,
Plus with all these pills
There's nothing left inside my pants.
Turning the t.v. on is practically like climbing a steep hill.

*Madness: a form of love*

Privilege and iniquity,
Two forces in fixed enmity.

Cancelling out our pathos.

I look around me, and see the world's sweat, blood, and tears,
Is spent on trinkets, and 5th holiday homes
For those passing a few most miserable years,
Too sick from depravity to reside in them.
Billions squandered on mimicking melanasome,
While the pale soul gathers dust, with nary an 'amen'.
Women careering too recklessly to care for her mother's aching bones,
And fathers flying too high to read stories to their children.

As for the millions starving in Africa- they can all rot.
Isn't that right, you greedy old sot?
The meat industry? It's swell.
Well done-you've created a living hell!
But its foolish to condemn, truly, I suppose,
We who suffer from it most are ourselves,
Its just the way that the wind, it blows,
We are destined to die the ironic, unlovely death of fallen angels.

Max J. Lewy

## A Power-Above

I bare my heart of my sleeve;
He pretends to snooze through it.
So what if I 'blew it' ?
It's only me that curses when we leave.

It doesn't matter to him.
Whereas my fate is limned by fear,
He is as heartless as he is artless.

What are my petty assaults to the ear,
Compared to that poisoned, incarcerated year ?
To a heavy horror that is forever near?

Do you think I should strive for a power-above?
Restrain my tongue, and, as they say, "hold it, bruv".

My wiliness says:
"Play Socrates to his Thrasymachus".
When justly scathing, his foolishness never fractures.

"Keep your friends close, and your enemies closer."
But since when must kin be enemies, and I
So surreptitiously puff up the old dozer ?

Do I keep it all in like a mouse,
As if I didn't truly belong in this house?

Better to shout it out loud and proud
While my emotions are still allowed.
Otherwise I may yet explode with this load.

Only where there is mutual honesty and understanding,
Can a home, at the top of that arduous staircase, have a pleasant landing.

Like a madman trying to reason with his shrink,
(telling him the truth that his treatments don't work,
even though the shrink will only redouble them as a result)

By our forceful tirades,
We show never wavering faith
In the power of Truth and Love.

I dream - (is it just a dream? Or has it already been...) -

That one day, some place, someone will finally be ready to view with joyful recognition and empathy the compassionate flames in the eyes of such a ferocious dove.

That, at least, would be essential to my criteria of a "power-above."

Max J. Lewy

## Our Own Great Missed Opportunity

Like a heavy boulder rolling inevitably down a stony hill,
We shall soon lay smashed in the valley even more dead,
Dare it be said; and remain there forever- perfectly still.

There was never a single sincere emotion we ever felt,
Except the dread, of our one great missed opportunity.

*Madness: a form of love*

# Rose Towards The Sun

Consciousness is the lens by which the Will attains focus,
Also the duct and channel through which it might freely flow.
It is the vessel, the very locus
That enables us to transcend and grow.

By keeping a watchful eye on where our energy is headed,
By all accounts, we will soon be wedded,
To the stars above and gods below.

The force inside;- so fierce, so spry.
Goodbye to all that wondering why.

A life of free inquiry awaits,
Such are the blessed pearly gates,
For he who with the eternal ideas- the Forms, mates.

For all mortal things, nothing but pity;
A little hatred at first, that keeps things gritty.
Dominate, beguile, cheat, subdue -
This, friends, is our earthly cue !

Inwardly, the Holy Spirit lifts us up,
(By golly, call me a nun...)
Climbing its way through the dark...
A rose... Arose towards the sun.

Max J. Lewy

## He Cometh No More

Beep, beep, beep...
The nurses check his life-support;
The fundees refuse to turn it off.

Christ returned but he was hit by a truck and is in a coma...
The d0ctor has an excellent diploma -
With nanotech he'll live for aeons.. as a vegetable.

How can He be reborn if He's not allowed to die...?
Alas, He cometh no more.
Satan wins.

*Madness: a form of love*

# Become Mentally-Ill And Make a Quick Buck

Oh! My poor brain,
Pray, this petty dupe to detain:
I fear I've gone, I've gone quite insane!

Bipolar, schizophrenia, depression - I've come down
with it all. Oppositional defiant disorder, ADHD, and so much more!
My father's fixed furrowed frown
Has crawled into places great and small.
I am bent, I am spent, I am rent
Six different ways.

I am meant, I am lent, I am sent
Into various dissarays.

Deliver me from my sickness, deliver me from it all,
Deliver me from the world, deliver me from the cure!

I am a pawn to play with,
I'll make somebody very rich -
Just not the taxpayer,
She's my little bitch.

I'll play the sad part,
Its written in the stars.
Scour the Infowars,
Making a new start?

I never was, but since you insist, now I am 'insane';
This is the best way I can derive my gain.
Your interventions have mortified my mind,
Yet kept from bouncing all the cheques I've signed.

God save the public purse!
Yes, I am a parasite;
But sucking on your blood
Is scant recompense for putting up with your blight.

Max J. Lewy

\*\*\*

Nothing left but to sit here and sing,
About the quaint dignity of living on the 'lunatic' wing!
Of putting up with all the phoney sanctimonious looks,
Of those behind all those big frowning medical books.

We are justified because of our plight.
We are justified because you are in the wrong,
And that makes us in the right.

There is something beautiful, something pure, something true,
About barely surviving the things that are wrought by you.

We are justified because we are still of worth,
There is still so much love and potential,
In those you rob of their rebirth.

We are all virtues, that eschew drab everyday conformity,
We are the Soul, that goes beyond narrow practicality.

And I am a piece of wonder, a living absurdity, a marvelous mistake,
That plays tricks on the minds of those unawake.

I shouldn't be able to write, yet I am;
I should be incapable of even a semblance of Reason,
According to your 'scientific' plan.

Sometimes I am a manic street preacher, with a piercing light in his eye,
That satirizes the shibboleths of your pious lie.

I shouldn't be able to think, yet I do;
I should be incapable of rendering a verdict,
On whether or not to live I am too blue.

Sometimes I am the Village Idiot, sometimes I am a new born child,

Madness: a form of love

Who foolishly tells the truth, however taboo or wild.

Now they call that too 'insanity';
They used to call it 'honesty'.
Is it so wrong that I want more than a quick buck?
That I aspire to more than to grab and then duck?
Does the fact that I have more than base gain in mind,
My message undermine, or my veracity incline?
Is it so wrong that I want a kinder society, and to live with pride?

The moon in June, halos with prescience;
'Lunatic' is the name of my sacred conscience!

*

Nothing left but to sit here and sing,
About the quaint dignity of living on the 'lunatic' wing!
Of putting up with all the phoney sanctimonious looks,
Of those behind all those big frowning medical books.

Of playing their game,
Of learning how to feign,
After that's what socialization is;
'Helping to flourish'? -
Thank you, but I'll sooner give that a miss!

"I know this may come as a surprise to you,
But I'm O.K. by myself.
And I don't need you,
And your 'benevolence' to save me...
And I never have! I never have. "

In poetry, thank God, there still might be a place,
For us who are otherwise treated as a sub race.

So: fight the stigma, fight it with all your might;
Because its nothing but labels,
Put there by those with Might but no Right!

So: fight the stigma, but don't fall for the disease,
 Its just a big charade your pockets to fleece!

Don't make the mistake of telling your loved ones they are ill,
 Especially, don't fall for the lie they can be cured by a pill;
 This is a self-fulfilling prophesy that cheats us even still.

Sometimes people need attention,
 Sometimes people need support.
 Sometimes it can, and sometimes it can't be bought.

But, either way, I beseech you

- And don't think I'm just making fun...

When I say...

Renew your faith in the 'talking cure',
 And in the ability of Love and Reason,
 To yet conquer all.

Then save a small ditty, have an ounce of pity,
 Don't stint now on the charity, for those like me,
 **Who were cast and branded in chemical chains in this 'Land Of the Free'.**

*Madness: a form of love*

# A Universal Song

Sentenced to vibrate to the beat of a Universal Song,
We are chained here, trapped forever and all along.
Everything that exists is eternally palpating with lamentation,
Behind the impenetrable bars that ring
And sing with tears and desperate gesticulation
The circumference of our Being, which is unable to bring Within it
The stars and lineaments of our innermost Longing,
Of our deepest hopes wrung from our lips with uttermost desolation.

The dazzling, pristine droplet of sunrisen dew that bedecks the Lily flower,
and holds within the apparent promise of all blessings, is... ?
The pupil says 'Divine?'
The Master yells,
"Worthless! "

We sit at the surface seams where we continue, sadly, to strum;
Hoping there is a way out, or from.
Or that our strings won't fray
When we are hung by a final chord, on Judgement Day.
At which grave hour, the scales will portray...
How much our miseries, our woes do weigh.
Then, unto eternity, shall on our broken hearts this ditty mockingly play?
On all our beautiful schemes and dreams Forever
Shall there echo, shall there hymn the enraged refrain of Never?
Into what am I henceforth thrown?
Nothingness is made quite appealing when you can do nothing but moan.
But, for our sins, in this mortal cage we do Sing;
In our requiem, we become One with the Everything,
Reaching beyond our personal Hell;
A good dirge makes Life surge as well.

Max J. Lewy

## Pill Puppet Poet

I am the pill puppet poet;
Fetid pharmacy's
Been forced down my gullet:

"Prophet of lunacy -
His days grey as a mullet-
Seeks for clemency
In ode or sonnet."

# Grief

Grief has its own grandeur. Weeping has its *sweep*. But penury and niggardliness of spirit... that is *true* damnation.

Hurled into this world, we all are. Given no choice, no option as to our family, our country, our creed, our intelligence, face or physique, or whether we even wanted to be born at all. We are but stones tossed upon the tide, to sink or to skim, to buttress an underwater Kingdom or consort with sea urchins, who knows what our fate will hold? As we grow, we attempt to reconcile ourselves to such fateful dispensations, either facing them with stern implacable acceptance or deluding ourselves that there is some 'higher plan' carefully provided for by an all loving, all wise, almighty ruler hidden behind the deceptive and confusing outer-fabric we call 'reality'. If we are lucky and are not struck down prematurely by some thunderbolt or other, or thwarted by the extreme malignancy of circumstances, we begin to carve out a small dominion upon this otherwise vexed and perplexing planet. We straddle our countless cares with a stray sunbeam here or there, dousing our ferocious, incipient fever of incomprehension with the sleek, refreshing wet flannel of facts and logic, and, (again, if we are lucky), adding a spoonful of honey, soothing for our sensitive tonsils, to the pot of cold, lumpy porridge we are given to imbibe. Like oysters, we begin to nurture, concealed deep within our souls, a little precious pearl of satisfaction amongst all the salty sorrow that invariably surrounds and often seems to drown us like an ocean of despair. Sometimes, we even forget about this encompassing infinity of woe altogether... and almost immediately, we begin to lose ourselves, our compass, our bearing, so that, as we amble nonchalantly and haughtily towards our next 'adventure', we end up tripping over a rock and hurtling head first, promptly breaking our necks. Then, our skulls are diligently trodden in by our 'rescuers'... Before we know it we are reduced to a tiny fraction of the much resented meagre portion which was first granted us, which suddenly in retrospect seems so very abundant, luscious, Edenic.

Like a cynosure of perfection, it calls out to us over the misty, miserly and beleaguered years we have known, beckoning us mournfully into its all-salving, but now irretrievably lost embrace. How we lean towards it, like a forsaken plant towards a distant, gleaming star... how we lovingly coo over it like the mother of a lost, sweet child... lift our hands imploringly to it as if we ourselves were beggars, or toast to it like an old comrade in arms... bargain with it like thieves before the jury, get down on our knees and pray to it like pilgrims, attempt to coax it from its hardened husky shell of passing years...But alas, to no avail. On our lips thenceforth forever, shall echo the engaged refrain of 'Never!'.

Yes, true damnation. True Hell. If only we had tended our sorrow earlier, if only we had sown the seeds in the harsh, melancholy fields of our youth; ploughed them with all our strength, with all our bitter fiercely loving dolorous rueful tears. How strong we would have been then, how we would have avoided all hiccups and set backs such as that little pebble over which we tumbled and cracked open our pitiless callow skulls spewing our brains across the most beautiful Persian rug in existence. But no, it wasn't to be. Instead of sowing seeds, we popped pills. Instead of ploughing our fields, we abraded our loins. Instead of tending our crop, we scatted salt in our own wounds.

So, now we must reconcile us not only to a life that we did not choose originally, but also to the loss of that original life which now seems so idyllic in comparison with the barren leftovers in its wake. Grief has its own grandeur. Weeping has its sweep, indeed. But, we are left only with blandness. Only with blunt brutish rude apathy and ennui. How I long to expire. To fade away imperceptibly into nothingness. To make a quiet, discreet exit from this terrible ignominious scene that has become my Life. If you want to turn a life into such a scene, turn them over to the doctors. If you want to make somebody beg, beg for sheer mercy and relief from what is being done to them... Get your white coat on, needle out, and start injecting away. Poison the heart of forever.

## Cherub Rock

The susurrating sea, it glistens;
In this place an angel listens,
Caressing your hair's every lock,
Down by the beautiful Cherub Rock.

Dreams take wing and fancy soars;
The tides echo around the shores,
For eons they have glittered and shook,
Down by the blessed Cherub Rock.

In this place the world forsook,
A secret lies in every nook,
Through the valley, by the brook,
Down by the crag of Cherub Rock.

Once upon some golden morrow,
Came from the sky the god Apollo,
And for a bride, a local beauty took,
Down by the nape of Cherub Rock.

Oh she was a maid so wan and fair,
A glittering jewel so very rare,
A fortunate fate for any man to defrock,
Down by the verdant Cherub Rock.

Soon, after nights sweet and wild,
She became ripe, full with child.
Mighty Apollo, he with triumph shook,
Down by the fateful Cherub Rock.

For a moment she seemed finally happy-
At one with life, this blessed lady.
Giving the crowds a glowing smile,
She danced throughout all Cherub Isle.

Max J. Lewy

Love so strong brings strange things...
The infants arrived- Siamese Twins.

And on their back, they had little wings...

It gave their parents quite a shock,
Down by the innocent Cherub Rock.

A physician arrived, he knew best;
How from one the other the babes to wrest-
How their pinions to nip and tuck,
Down by the watchful Cherub Rock.

But, by Heaven, the plan went wrong,
Young mother, in tears to a funeral song.
Bathed in infant blood, the trees all shook,
Down by the pitiless Cherub Rock.

For years the young bride pined away,
Apollo, from sorrow, he couldn't stay.
It seems a love so wild and free,
Could but end in calamity.

Finally she threw herself
Clinging to their coffin, off the cliff-
Caressing their hair's every lock,
As she fell from the beautiful Cherub Rock...

The susurrating sea, it glistens;
In this place a dead angel listens,
Caressing your hair's every lock,
Down by the *cursed* Cherub Rock.

## Crystal Carrion

And the blood red sea,
The ghosts of tomorrow;
And my heart pumping, listlessly,
And the birds of sorrow...

And the pit of fire in my gut,
And the fumes let off from
The holes in my head...
And the small pond of ice,
That lays still, as I lay still in bed.

(This-time tomb of tadpoles, one-month mirror of maypoles...)

The cold, cold ice, with crocuses
Blooming, purple as my veins, crowned.

Next brittle skeleton trees, with hovering fingers
Pointing accusingly into the wind...

All of them, FLOWERS STREWN,
By an all-knowing, unseen hand?

And the surrounding, frost-painted grey-emerald grasses...
And the freezing wet air, breathing like smoke through the rushes...
Which wave nonchalantly like rolled cigarettes
Between His shivering, almighty digits...

The wide open skies reflected,
In this crystal carrion,
Of Spring's less favoured conjoined sister.

Max J. Lewy

# The Great Invisible

Did you suspect the quark, in the dark knit-work of matter?
Did you unravel the mysteries of the pyramids?
Did you guess the coral, seahorse and pearl, in the waters deep?

Did you identify the drowning children behind their desks?

Did you glimpse the nuclear explosions of the sun?
Did you see the malice behind the sparkling smile of the nun?
Did you watch the radiation give the village cancer?
Did you know that shy girl would grow up to be a pole dancer?

Did you sense that as below, so above?
Did you weep for the 'worms' killed by the 'dove'?
Did you see him slowly destroyed by the secret parasite in his gut?
Were you the one who helped the drunkard out of that rut?
Did you imagine the diamonds in the black coal of filthy hillside?
Didn't you say there's nothing behind the surface of the mind?

Didn't you invite the Trojan Horse into the city?
Didn't you say at the crucifixion? 'goodbye poor man, that was a pity!'

99.9% of life is invisible.
And yet you think you have me all cut and dried?

# A Parable, 'Man And Truth'

There was once a man with the true teaching on Life - the keys to Enlightenment and happiness beyond most people's wildest comprehension. It applied to almost everyone except himself. Unfortunately, not only was it also beyond most people's comprehension, but whenever he tried to convey this teaching, only gibberish and sticky wet ash came out of his mouth. Furthermore, he was practically illiterate.

He prayed to God – or the devil – and asked him, 'O Lord, why have you given me this wonderful teaching with no one to listen to me and heed your Word?'.

The blessed, miserable old git spoke thus:

'For many years, you have carried this teaching within you, ripe for the benefit of all humanity – except yourself. Still, because you are not made to be an example, no one hearkened to your message. Worse, if you were foolish enough to go out preaching, you were regarded as merely a bloody fool, and were lucky if you escaped butchery for your pains, since only nonsense and sticky wet ash came out of your mouth. Thus, you endured only mockery and humiliation for what I have given you. Indeed, you were most vexed. But, though you are now old and will be gone soon, you still cling inextricably to your truth, to this awful agony..in such a way showing admirable self-reverence and loyalty.. though it proved of no use to yourself whatever and was in fact utterly futile. Thus should it be between every man and the Truth.'

# Orchid

A chill triumvirate of diadems,
Amid pirouettes of billowing mist,
Lit by black-laced thread.
Remembrance, the nightly detour
Of obsidian osmosis.

Watching your sweet heart palpate
Away, in dank, black uncelebrated shades.
Regret stands on every altar.
But -ah !-
Hijack the moon! -
You are my first and last

soliloquy.

Without lustre, lacking liberty,
Lanturne of laconic intermissions.
Listen! There flits a dragonfly,
On its way to the stars.

Lo ! A maniacal masquerade.

The play of the sleepwalkers;
Ghosts, with coffee-ed out souls...

We shiver together prone in the wind...
As a monsoon lifts her ankles,
And begins to waltz across the skies.

Tears of crystal, only friend.

## Gemini Asunder

Born June 18th,
Two halves, Max and Jim;
Inextricably linked,
Gemini twins.

One lay hidden,     One warily cocked his head above the parapet,
The other warily cocked his head above the parapet.    The other lay hidden.

They caught him in crooked net. Sawed off,    (They took advantage,
of behind his ears the wet.)

His secret genome bro. His shadow,
His adamantine heart, his right brain,
His subterranean soul.

Now, only a hollow shell of logic,
Urchin under watery grave -

We mechanical animals -
Let this be pedagogic:

You tyrants can never repay this inextricable deprave.

## Unmetabolizable Angst

Not a passing congestion of the blood,
Not a stifling restriction of the breath.
Such affects merely come and go;
How unlike my woe.

More of a submerged, yet sovereign blight,
Immaculately encased in, and preserved,
By a soft fatty tissue of years;

Undoing every scheme, in amniocentesis.
A quiet seething, a thwarted satisfaction;

Decades of distress, rendered solid, permanent;
Enveloping and encumbering,
Infiltrating the very nerves.

Like a nuclear power-station,
I am the seat of untold reactions,
Harnessing the energy of the atomic individual.
But, I have a hole, a lack, a fatality.

A leak...

Imbued upon me by a mere boypage!
This is the unrequited scar, I call my 'rage'.

And I am destined to irradiate this world,
In want of clarity, with my charity.

I love the little mice, so meek to inherit,
The alopecia love with which I sterilize.
To wake in the morning, in lieu of merit,
Takes all my powers of self-hypnosis.

Where is the warrior? Where is the dove?
Long live the King, for me this world is snuffed.

Madness: a form of love

# Never mind

Never mind that the light has grown dim,
Never mind that our dreams have grown ghostly thin,
Never mind that we are being poisoned to death,
'Never mind' I say with my last breath.

Never mind that the cops are gunning us down,
Never mind that we drop like flies without a sound.
Never mind that the prisons are over-flowing,
And that life itself has become a prison,
In which, like cattle, we are mournfully lowing.

Never mind that the nurses have become our jailers,
We who once dreamt of becoming such cosmic sailors.
Never mind that they surely impale us
One little needle at a time.

It is useless to rake up a fuss;
For us its too late, we've already missed the bus.
I feel stupid and contagious-
Now, entertain us!

We sure do need one hell of a party.
O please! Take off your panties.
Like Truth, you are most ravishing when dressed scantily.
O, don't you rant at me! You are all ants to me!
Let's party like it was 2099, surveying the universe
From a great precipice.
Come, join me with the 'Transhumanist's Manifesto' as we piss on this!
Let it all burn, burn, burn!
I do admire with what cruelty, what boldness me you spurn...
But it is after all your clumsy, cross-eyed sister for whom I do yearn!
Let me dance with her by moonlight mit violin until my feet
Are bloody and swollen from her ungainly trod-Marx!
(Only those who's role-models are 19th century German
corpses have this intoxicating aroma!)

Max J. Lewy

We shall expire together on this Satanic balcony,
As the world explodes. Panting, parched and hungry for life;
Calling out, 'Da Capo!' 'Da Capo!'
'Grandiose-delusions', you say? Watch it, or you'll get a slap-o.

## Note To The Homeless

Blessings and gratitude to you, our stray sons
and daughters of the streets. With each cupped palm,
you make my riches reach a higher relief, juxtaposed
to the verdant, mottled valley of your thousandfold poverty
and picturesque surrender, like the march of holy men
and the many prophets before you.

For how many centuries have you lain amongst us, nestled beneath your rags on the corners of our ancient Polis, in the front square by the statues of our gods and goddesses or the great men of yesteryear, to today under prepossessing, store-front verandas, gathering your slowly ripened and hard fought wisdom? Were you not here long before us, in the far-away time when the world was still young?

Are you not the ocean depths, to which all currents eventually flow in and out of, being once again reborn in humility and awe, as passing dust before the sublime infinity, which renders us all as beggars before the mighty One and All
?

Ah yes, you were here long ago. You are no petty plaything of fate, or stooge to be exploited, like some think. Rather, you are the archetype of our primordial past, we who crawled from dust and thereto shall return. You rekindle our lust for self-betterment, for the conquest of this miserly nature; re-asserting our primal, authentic instincts in the light of the abandonment to the elements. He who scorns you shows to all and sundry his vulgar self-seeking petty limited cave-like valuations, a slave to the herd.

Speak no more, my tongue! You prize panthers of the urban jungle do not need my praise or defense; you know all this in your bones, confronting your critics with only child-like curiosity, humble, good-hearted, stoical acceptance and occasional, non-comprehending shake of the head.

Be brave, be stalwart, above all, be patient with us mere propertied normies – we who are ourselves the property of our property to the precise degree to which we own it - for one day we shall return amongst you with only an empty
vase and foolish look in our eyes, as a forsaken and wayward child, who longs only for reconciliation.

Max J. Lewy

## "Schizophrenia" will demean ya

I am a fake, I am a fraud,
Take me seriously, and we'll all be very bored.
I am an Emperor with no clothes,
I am a charlatan, I am the enemy of those
I lead by the nose.
My name is the cause of all your woes,
All I do is fatten the greediest of sows.
My bearers are little battered Christs arisen,
Whom I crucify anew with every fresh prescription.
To convince you you're insane, that is my mission.
To insidiously, self-righteously lay blame, that's my decision.
Dionysus, that divine lunatic, ripped to pieces.
And at the expense of the taxpayer, my work cunningly fleeces.
To stigmatize those who flout convention,
And render them in indefinite detention.
In a living Hell because of their dissention,
And other cruelties which I don't care to mention.
Men and women in white coats, these are my henchmen.
Once I get through with you, your soul will slobber,
And never stop drooling and whining like a servile dog in heat,
As it gets beat, before its new sadistic Master's feet...

Schizophrenia, it will demean ya!

*Madness: a form of love*

# Asylum Chums

Sentenced to grieve for a hundred years, recurring eternally.
Pacing the wards with a head full of pain, condemned infernally.
Then, I watch it wave. Who is this nuisance?
For once I am in no mood for romance.

Talking tentatively amidst the tentacles of State,
I try for moment to withhold my hate.
I look at the ground, I heave a sigh,
I hope they're not gonna my brain ta fry.

Oh truly, I want to cry,
I'd be better off dead.
But when she saw Pascal's 'Pensees' in my pocket;
"Its a miracle", she said!

- But are there still miracles in Hell? -

Oh, and to think, she actually claims to like these meals;
As for me, I'd sooner down a jar of slime-infested pickled eels!
Oh, get me out of here! Oh, how I wish!
At least there is now someone who speaks The Queen's English!

But reading 'Being and Time' together was scant consolation,
For all the Time I was Being on medication.
The 'Nothing noths', oh yes, that I understand well!
It is precisely the stuff that these fine Dr.s sell.

Moral scruples, I have a few;
But they're fading quickly,
As my thoughts turn only to revenge.
This one here, seeks the Holy Grail.

Obsessive compulsive, paranoid schizophrenic;
These doctors have labels much less than Edenic!

I consider them simply 'moronic'.

This patient requires patience,
I try to be as patient as I can.
But I know deep down,
She suspects I'm a very bad man!

We are all grave sinners,
Her 'especially'.
Frankly I don't feel that guilty...
(I was only just getting going!)

I strangely admire her ability to sweet talk the other inmates, envy it perhaps.
I pity them too, but in such a state myself I am incapable of much kindness.
I hope she knows I have good intentions.

What? Released before me? Oh God, the tart!
Talk about putting the lucky apples, before the poor cart!
What am I supposed to do now? She was the only one mildly alert!
Forgive me, my friend – I'm only teasing. Mu ha ha ha !
**Happy birthday, dear Jemimah! Here is to old times...**
**Hip! hip! Hurrah !**

## The Mask Is No More

Pantomime mask laying spent on the debris-ridden floor,
No mystery left unturned, no surprises from me anymore.

All fuel of this once-glittering fire used-up, burned.
"Why" I wonder, does my body not yet expire ?
My soul has committed the ultimate blunder.
It shall never again flash with lightening, or sound
With thunder: to abash and amaze this tight-laced
World with its disarming "candour", to wave its wand
And daze and confuse with a new passing ruse-
To leave fazed and crazed with the "out-pouring"
Of my muse. The warring faction of my heart
Has let heave a fatal sigh. It has raised the white
Flag, and for that it will most surely have to die.
The mind is truly spent, when it loses the will to lie.

Max J. Lewy

# Holy Land

A Palestinian girl and a Jewish boy wrestled for hours,
Then festooned each other with garlands of flowers.
Two Semites realized that the Holy Land
Was wherever the other one was standing...
Then God came down from 'up there'
And planted bombs in their underwear.

## My Lost Israel

O, tear-stain of temerity! Filch the stars from the sky!
Where hast thou gone, mine clarity? How oft' do I sigh...
How often do they lie... How often must I fry...

Mausoleum of merriment, sarcophagus of spin;
Thy impunity of impudence, hath verily done me in!
Oh what a slight..what a sin!.. Hail the looney bin!

A mark of macabre mal-intent, by such spineless hacks,
However can I withstand, the quailing, underhand attacks...
Of this pack of low-down quacks!!!

\*\*\*

Fractious entrails, of society's spayed organism.
Sunk in chains, art we, to their unholy catechism.

Max J. Lewy

# The Call Of Duty

With such beguiling panache, the dashing flash of my electronic screen
Connects me with countless players. Our pale faces florescently reflect its hypno-beam.
The amplifier booms brashly out from its box;
In the images I watch,
My target surreptiously locks;
And in its sure grip I myself am imprisoned.

Murdering millions of AI, medallions line my scrollbar.
In reality, too oblivious to realize I'll die,
Too feckless to even begin to see what I might try.
Entertainment is my favourite enslavement.

Conformist without a cause; I abide by most laws,
But have never heard of Plato's "The Laws"; a good book merely bores.
Nor am I aquaint with the constitution; I resign my rights- slow diminution.
And always, I expect to be let off scot free, by the reassuring call... the 'Call Of Duty'!

## Thoughts Of The Unborn

So, finally, I AM.
I am ! The universe is alive.
It's my mum.
The world is a throbbing hive,
And I am the Queen bee.
It is made to comfort me.

A multiform, rippling tapestry of veins and nerves,
Support and nourish each of my incipient verves.
It has been like this since the first moment I can remember,
I suck from a cord in my tummy,
And am granted sustenance so warm and yummy!

There is little need to cheat or dissemble.
No need to pretend I'm not hurt, by the lies that you assert,
And the chemicals that you insert.

I know you love me.

Still, with each new passing day,
My hunger grows without delay.
I have already learned to wage war
For the sake of having more, more, more.

I summon my strength and send out signals of distress
Letting life know
It must make expiations for getting me in this sticky mess.

I sit snugly in this little patch,
And snatch and snatch and snatch.

Still, it usually yields to the pinings my will wields.

Somehow... I have this dream of wide-open fields,

Max J. Lewy

Starry skies, hopes that penetrate beyond all whys.

But even now, I can already smell my necessary demise.

Just as I now joyously grow, soon, I can sense it,
I will be over-run by woe. My existence is a piece of
Brute injustice, of which I am both victim and
perpetrator, righted only by the decomposition of
Passing years.

So let it not shock you, if I mark my new arrival with...

Much blood, and many tears!

## **Mountain Path**

Lain carved into the mountainside,
Spiralling its way, through the mist,
A path no more than a meter wide,
  Like the fading notes of Liszt.
An eagle circles, her chicks cried;
  If I should fall, no one to assist.

Fleet foot,
Cloaked hood;
I scale without remorse.
Magical aetites stone,
Awaits for me, of course.

I intone a spell, by the grand ravine.
I stutter a prayer, with all my spleen.

There is something beyond,
What the low-land folk speak.
It revolves all around
A heavily shrouded peak.

The world goes on; it doesn't care;
Oblivious to my hatchings of fate.
Rare sights, strange vistas; beware!
Fire and brimstone, avalanche hate.

## **Rain Panegyric**

The many besmirch the downpour,
alienating the likes of me from their
affections. We live on different plains -
though we may share an uneasy

facile companionship, our souls are
nourished by opposite elements. They
worship the sun, I bask in the deluge.
Why wield an umbrella, when a little

drizzle refreshes and does no harm?
Why such cursing and alarm? Why
run-indoors, as if the same substance
of which we are mostly formed, was a

plague of locusts to be abhorred ? In
reality, this royal torrent is the pure,
life-giving nectar with which this earth
is restored; a salutary, blessed dose

of the very Heavens, letting us dance in
abandonment to its super-terrestrial,
dewy abundance.

Perhaps secretly
what I long for is the Flood which will

cleanse the earth of your testing malice
towards all that does not offer up its glow,
like a smiling orb, high in the sky, but
rather hangs back in unusual, strange,

darkened places; tentative, damp corners
of this earth, wherein such shade it can

escape the distorting effects of the mass
gaze. Watching the wild rain come in from

its hallowed perch, it will flow just the same,
imperviously, twisting serpentine streams in
staunch wet-eyed openness, towards the
sacred soil of its own furtive, star-distant

ideal.

Max J. Lewy

## Tears Of Solace

Gravel paths line the way, to my abode of the fey.
Rough surface, heavy footsteps, stones of grey.
With weary spirit, I scale them day-after-day.

How I pray my blisters bloom!
One fine day in Love's high-noon.
But between you and me,
Always just out of reach, 'twill be.

Yet, in the corner of this pale yard,
Situated in a small, bleak pond.
I look inside, and what do I see?
Droplets of solace, there for me.

Melancholy home, thoughts wandering-
Roam, by me only known...Vistas they bring.

Upon lilies growing there deep in;
Tears flowing, free from sin.
A lonely spot, in day or night,
Keeping my soul still barely alight.

## Monsoon Bride: (Or, I Refuse to Hurt)

The sun fled its make-shift throne,
Retreating to safety, in exile,
While the planets plotted and began offing
One another in the lofty palace of the sky,
From whence long shadows did fall.

Mother earth buckled and clawed herself asunder,
From sheer fear, as the clouds hovered in
Eerie, grim portent, before releasing a tide
of pelting rain upon her naked back.

I wanted to flash my demented, palpating eyes
In the face of the pious; I want to scream
like a bird of prey, or the poor, despairing wretch
Under its talons. I wanted to
Leap off the side of the earth and break
free of its suffocating gravity.

But, I just stood still, because I knew,
To give an inch would be to give a mile.
To break now would be never more to smile.
So, I just let the torrent bleed
Itself wantonly and pitilessly about me,
Refusing to permit it to weaken my spirit.
I held myself like as a witness,
As an avatar, and people crowded
Around from near and far,
As the dim lantern of my soul
Sustained itself though the fog,
Though the ice, through the tests,
Trials and tribulations
That were now at hand,

And began to brace itself
For those that were yet to come.
Never more to yield, never more to flail,
Never more to give in. This is my faith,
This is the way we atone for our sin.

Not to get down our knees,
Not curse ourselves in rank obeisance,
But to hold strong through the storm,
Our own creation, a product of our own
Malice and despair against ourselves.

To wail? So selfish.
To bawl? So callow.
Too many souls in distress,
Too much work to be done,
Too much pride to defend,
To wallow deeper in this mess.

On the obverse, with perverse
And unbending will, we embrace
Our own destiny, our own dessert,
Our own wretched yet divinely-ordained
And erotically necessary - harshly beautiful -
Imperious, yet demure, in her recalcitrant
Obstreperousness to be ridden in...

**OUR UNFATHOMABLY MYSTERIOUS, MONSOON BRIDE.**

*Madness: a form of love*

# Backstreet Buddha (Lets fall a jewel...)

I swipe the pockets of the rich;
Relieving them a little of there material burdens.
Without a care, I snitch,
On all society's would-be guardians.
Sitting here, in this ditch,
Having remarkable conversations...
I am a pariah, a wicked witch;
Setting his own conflagrations.

Beauty, blessedness, repartee;
Flows in my blood, animates my bones.
As footfalls clatter urgently on these cobblestones...
The sidewalk is my very own settee.
Your funny lives, my T.V.!

Roam the land, sniff the air;
Falling golden silent, I kneel and stare...

Thinking quietly to myself...

"This old world, it will soon be forgotten.
My gown may be dirty,
My skin may be swarthy...
But, also? My Ego ist Toten!

Everything changes, you see,
Everything changes like the river to the sea,
Everything changes, from the shores of Italy,
To the borders of Greece and Turkey.

As, yes, Deutchland falls,
And with it Europe, too.
Your consumer kingdom is dead;
Who am I to wail?

An old god says 'Boo!'.

# Relics

Ancient relics stand taller
Than when they were new
Just like my battered mind
They shatter with dignity
As for those who despoil
What insults their vanity
Those who sniff at liberty
Scattering their own guts
Across the wailing desert
Or pills down our throats
Gloating in raw domination
Their ghostly spirits depart
From this world in rank
And profane ignorance
Destined forever to vanish
Never again to see sunrise
But our sacred city and
Even our souls one day may
For they are built of Love

## **Blitzcare**

Yes officer, what dose should I take?
I've seen men's limbs sprayed and flayed,
my comrades rendered wide by landmines.
I've held my breath neck deep in mud as

enemy soldiers prowled meters away
whilst every inch of me wanted to scream.
I've marched for over a week without sleep.
I've done as you ordered, though it was beyond

me to endure. Now, I put my trust in you to
relieve me of my burdens. But, what is this
restless state in which I'm cast? What are these
hallucinations, this unquenchable thirst? Didn't

you say these drugs would heal me? But now I'm
impotent as well as lame. I wake in the
night with cold sweats, trembling; nothing
brings me joy. For God and country,

I was willing to die. I put my faith in you.
But now you destroy my mind. You leave
me tattered and torn in a loony bin. Do you
want to shut me up? So that others won't learn

The terrible truth about war? It would have
been kinder had I died on the front. This
betrayal stings worse than any shrapnel.
Wasn't my sacrifice and dedication enough?

Max J. Lewy

## He Strove

He strove against the world, and all the lethargy it contains,
The doleful march of men unable to see beyond their little lanes.
He strove against the moon, Relentless ruler of the tide,
He swore that when his fate'd come, he'd be ready just in time;
He strove against the land, the air, the sun, the sea,
The little folk who laugh, and throw stones at you and me;
He strove against the grain, he strove against the sand,
He hoped to build a magic fortress and do it all by his mind;
He strove against the pull, he strove against the tow, - Of a thousand years
-
He said that its the stubbornest men, who have the best careers.
He strove so long, so hard, so proud, against shallow conformity,
The sorry thing was, - so exhausted with striving was he - he never did leave his dormitory!

## Paralysed By The Prick Of A Dovetail

Your retiring presence
And silent beauty
Torments me to my essence
It becomes my solemn duty
To be lacerated through
By your whispers true.

I beg you, stay loyal to this image,
Never vulgarize yourself with idle prattle.
You are a Queen, and I am your revering chattel.

With such subtle violence.
You invade my soul,
Giving me sweet licence,
To be beside myself with woe.
If only you knew
The power inside you.

Always keeping my distance,
Unwilling to accept your
Concern, I never learn.

You prove the myth of Medusa to be false,
It is grace, not ugliness, that freezes the pulse.

I cannot rest until our spirits together nail,
Paralysed by the prick of a dovetail.

I long for the purity
Of mutual admiration,
Mercilessly unmingled
By human pity.
But I make no moves to achieve it,
I can't be very witty.

Max J. Lewy

About you I could never laugh...
I am but your still photograph.

You are as pale and quiet as the Moon,
Should I not be as brazen and warm as the Sun?
But I am merely your own reflection,
Your would-be clone in troubled waters.

You are like me,
And I want to become more like you.
But, you make me forget, I must go my own way too.

To me you are a priestess, an ancient tomb,

I belong inside you
Where I could grow like flowers
That I might festoon around your milk-white throat
The birth-place of so many maddening susurrations.

You are less a person than a surrogate God.

## Lost In The Fray

Hero of battle without medallions,
Crushed beneath stampeding stallions
Of strife many years earlier.
Each new day, I awake and lay flowers
By the ramparts of my own grave,
Hoping by this small offering to save
A vestigial remnant of my soul;
Heaping cards of remembrance, I dole
Gratitude and bitterness upon the departed:
Our plans 'til eternity thwarted.
Stars withdrawing from the skies above,
Left with only a lunatic love...
Until nightfall when they sway back my way:
Illumining the ghost of a former man
So pale, uncanny and wan.
Recalling my pain, I'll lay here and pray
*Forever and ever, lost in the fray.*

Max J. Lewy

# Rivers Of Eternity (For R.W.)

Two rivers miraculously intertwine;   Two rivers miraculously intertwine;
Above our heads, the stars align.   Beneath our eyes, the dew doth shine.
In all our colorful sins, we are akin:   In all our excess glee, you and me.
Two happy lunatics- one broke free of the bin;   Two happy mad- one a dearly trapped fairy;
The other, his wild fantasies enabling.   The other, longing to set her free.

Love: a madness saner than sanity itself;
Dispensing knowledge like the Oracle at Delphi.
"Who is the wisest man in all the land? - Socrates"
He'll try his best to prove you wrong; never questioning cease.

Two rivers beautifully intertwine;   Two rivers beautifully intertwine;
My soul is yours, your heart is mine.   Words float upon lips, just like wine.
I'll try my best to prove you wrong;   I'll try my best to prove myself false;
Let slip the secrets I have held anon.   Even still, it quickens your pulse.
Yet still you hearken to my dark love song.   To my nostrils you are sweet balsam.

Love: a madness more sober than sobriety;
Studying, like Nietzsche, a science of gaiety.
"Thou goest to women? Forgetest not thine whip!"
And I place a lilac flower on your hip.

Two rivers majestically intertwine;   Two rivers majestically intertwine;

Madness: a form of love

I can be cruel, or I can be kind.   I can be crass, or I can be refined.
Whichever way, you may swoon;   You can be shy, or you can brim over;
At my infatuated words-passion of the moon:   I still feel luckier than a four-leaf clover:
Oh, how I long to cocoon you in my arms.   And, besides, my heart tires of being a rover.

Love: a madness more healing than the pill.
"Love is composed of a single soul inhabiting two bodies" - quoth Aristotle.
Into yours my river, and yours into mine, flows-
Carrying the bitter seeds, fallen from the rushes,

Through Fate's fearful marshes,
Which we both will downstream sow,
To make poppies of our past.